RIMBAUD

Illuminations

Roger Little

Professor of French,
Trinity College, Dublin

Grant & Cutler Ltd
1983

I.S.B.N. 84-499-6740-6
DEPÓSITO LEGAL: V. 2.752-1983

Printed in Spain by
Artes Gráficas Soler, S.A., Valencia
for
GRANT & CUTLER LTD
11 BUCKINGHAM STREET, LONDON W.C.2

Critical Guides to French Texts

29 Rimbaud: Illuminations

Critical Guides to French Texts

EDITED BY ROGER LITTLE, WOLFGANG VAN EMDEN, DAVID WILLIAMS

Contents

To Sam, 'suprême Savant', from one of the 'horribles travailleurs'; and to Pat, Dominic and Rebecca, who sacrificed a husband and father to make the work possible.

Prefatory Note

References to poems in the *Illuminations* are by their titles, so
that any good edition may be used, though I make recommend-
ations in the selective bibliography at the end of this volume.
References to works listed in that bibliography are by an itali-
cised number in parentheses, followed if appropriate by a page
number, e.g. (*15*, p.64). Quotations from the *Illuminations*
follow the text of the Bernard/Guyaux edition (*1*), departing
from it only where I have reason to believe from a perusal of the
manuscripts that some minor change should be made. For all
quotations from Rimbaud other than from the *Illuminations*,
reference is made to the latest Pléiade edition (*2*).

R.L.
Paris, October 1982

Proem

Nobody knows exactly when the *Illuminations*, any one of them, were written. Nobody knows the order of their composition nor the order Rimbaud — if indeed he was the author of every single one of them — might have chosen for their publication. Nobody knows if the collection we know as the *Illuminations* contains more texts than it should or less than it might have done. Nobody even knows whether *Illuminations* (and is it English or French?) is the title Rimbaud would have fixed on if he had seen his book through the press. Such swathes of ignorance help concentrate the mind wonderfully on the texts themselves.

Critics have often, of course, adopted other approaches: historical, sociological, ideological, graphological, alchemical, psychological, psychoanalytical, psychopathological and so forth, or Polonius-like permutations of such readings. They have thrown light on these frequently obscure *Illuminations*, and their contribution is far from negligible. The literary critic will never ignore it, but his preoccupation with texts, however widely it may range in search of better understanding, determines a refusal on his part: never to allow the text to become a mere pretext. The poem, like any work of art, stands at a crossroads between the assembled cerebral, emotional, experiential and expressive features of the poet confronting reality on the one hand and the same — inevitably different — totalising forces of his reader on the other.

If the text should not be a mere pretext, nor can it be solely a product of context. A deterministic notion of art, contrived extrinsically by what Taine called 'la race, le milieu et le moment', admits of no room for individual genius. The quest for textual autonomy, whereby a poem flies free of the circumstances of its making and of the confines of its maker, has been a feature of French poetic thinking over the last hundred years. It accepts and indeed welcomes the inevitable right of the reader to

make the text his own by seeing it in the light of his own inter-
pretation, so counteracting any tendency to fossilise the poem at
a moment in history and reacting against contextual
determinism. A sense of the eternal present arises only if a poem
is seen as successfully focussing the sources of its light and
making them radiate in arresting patterns for successive
generations of readers. This the *Illuminations* have
conspicuously succeeded in doing.

My metaphor of light waves, though, however apt for a
collection of poems entitled *Illuminations*, should not be taken
in any restrictive sense. Patterns of sound and syntax, striking
imagery and juxtapositions, resonances through connotations
and ambiguity, the very shape of a poem on the page, these are
only the more general features of the poet's strategy of which the
detailed tactics are so often obscured by seemingly impenetrable
technical terms.

Of one such tactic, familiar and so not burdened by jargon,
Rimbaud has willingly — some might say wilfully — deprived
himself in the *Illuminations*. He abandons the recurrent rhyming
patterns of traditional versification. Several important questions
arise from this fact, and will demand our attention later: Was it
from a sense either of his own inadequacy at writing verse or of
the inadequacy of the form to express his meaning? A retreat or
an advance not just for himself as a poet but also in the develop-
ment of our understanding of the nature of poetry? Can prose,
in fact, be poetry — rather than 'poetic', with the generally
pejorative implication of floridity, purple passages and
apparently uncontrolled spasms of logorrhoea? An analysis of
selected texts will, I believe, contribute towards positive answers
to these questions, and show Rimbaud as a uniquely stimulating
master of his craft. Much will remain unexplained: just like
other critics, I do not hold the key to this 'parade sauvage'
('Parade'), and even Rimbaud, having found it, was sub-
sequently to lose it... or throw it away. But in some ways I am
not sorry to leave the poetic mystery of the *Illuminations* intact
— a brilliant star surrounded by utter darkness, and not without
its own dark spots.

1. The Text and its Problems

The *Illuminations* are dazzling, and our critical pupils have to adjust to their brilliance; only then can we view them with some discernment. But our task is made harder because of the strobo-scopic effects of which Rimbaud is particularly fond: his texts pulsate, sometimes in a single throb, sometimes with more rapid successions of now-you-see-it now-you-don't images, seeming expansions and contractions of his mental space.

This being so, we are in the dark half the time, and our fear of the dark, akin to nature's abhorrence of a vacuum, leads us to try and fill in the picture, to rationalise the texts in as logical a way as is allowed by our experience of them, of Rimbaud's other writings, of what we know of his life, and of the whole socio-cultural context. That critics should be partial seems almost inevitable in the circumstances. They are drawn towards assumptions, towards the more or less tentative filling in of blanks, and while when we look through a venetian blind we complete the half-image of what lies beyond with a reasonable assurance of accuracy, that degree of probability is drastically reduced when a poet's imaginative leaps are the object of scrutiny. Rimbaud's use of ellipsis brings marvellous juxta-positions, but it can also leave us groping in the dark.

Our degree of certainty is reduced by the very way in which the texts have survived: we are lucky to have them at all (see *2*, pp.972-75).[1] From September 1871 to July 1873, Rimbaud and the poet Paul Verlaine, ten years his senior, led a wandering and dissolute life together, brought to an abrupt halt by a violent tiff in which Rimbaud was shot in the wrist. Released from prison, Verlaine went to see Rimbaud at Stuttgart for a couple of days in February 1875 and came away with instructions to convey a

---

[1] For greater detail and some hypotheses about the gaps in our knowledge on the matter, see Pierre Petitfils, 'Les Manuscrits de Rimbaud', *Etudes rimbaldiennes*, 2 (1970), pp.72-88.

batch of Rimbaud's prose poems to another poet friend then in Brussels, Germain Nouveau, with the aim of publication. Nouveau, who had probably first met Rimbaud in Paris in late 1873, left precipitately with him for London in March 1874 and quitted him, no less precipitately it seems, that June. According to a close graphological study of the manuscripts (see *34*), Nouveau helped Rimbaud copy out his text, being responsible for 'Villes' ('L'acropole ...') except for the title, and for part of 'Métropolitain' (from 'arqué' onwards) except for the word 'Guaranies', but this has been disputed (see e.g. *18*). For present purposes, I shall assume that all the texts are by Rimbaud, as I believe this, on existing evidence, to be the case. Whether the batch of prose poems that Verlaine sent to Nouveau in 1875 (he complains of the cost of their postage in a letter of 1st May and is likely to have posted them therefore not long before) constituted the whole of the *Illuminations*, or whether Nouveau already had some of them, or whether indeed Rimbaud had written all of them by then, all these are unknown factors, subject to the endless hypotheses of commentators.

For reasons again unknown, Nouveau did not publish the texts in Brussels. If he made any efforts in that direction and tried the printer M.-J. Poot who had published *Une saison en enfer* in 1873 but never been paid for his pains, one can understand why silence ensued. His own reluctance at having his name linked any more with that of Rimbaud, who had a reputation for irresponsibility in Parisian literary circles, not to mention the understandably poor view taken by Verlaine's estranged wife and her respectable family, may have played a part. In any case, at some time before 9 August 1878, when the title *Illuminations* figures for the first time, in a letter from Verlaine to his by then ex-brother-in-law Charles de Sivry, the latter had both received the manuscript (by an entitlement which remains obscure) and lent it to Verlaine, who declares that he has re-read them with pleasure:

Avoir relu *Illuminations (painted plates)* du sieur que tu sais [...]. Te le rapporterai vers octobre. Dangereux par les postes. Choses charmantes d'ailleurs, au milieu d'un tas de zolismes avant la lettre, par conséquent inavouables.

The danger of obscene material ('zolismes') being confiscated was perhaps as great as fortuitous loss. Verlaine returned the papers to Sivry as promised but lived to regret it, or at least to regret not having copied the texts, for no doubt with publication in mind he writes again and again to Sivry for their return: 'et les *Illuminécheunes*, donc!' (27 October 1878); 'Pourrais-tu, si tu as fini avec les *Illuminations* (*coloured plates*, etc...) lui confier le paquet dûment enveloppé à mes adresses?' Verlaine was never to see the manuscript(s) again, it would seem, for in 1886, Gustave Kahn, the editor of a lively young literary magazine, *La Vogue*, persuaded Sivry to part with them (through the agency of up to two intermediaries) and entrusted the editorial work on them not to Verlaine but to Félix Fénéon. After publication, the pieces of paper were split up and have remained scattered, some now being in public collections (at the Bibliothèque Nationale in Paris, the Bibliothèque Bodmer at Cologny near Geneva, and the Bibliothèque Municipale at Charleville, where Rimbaud was born in 1854), some in private hands, and others lost or mislaid.

Fénéon's work for *La Vogue* gave rise to two further complications. One is that the pages making up the batch which he had to edit were unnumbered and apparently random. The paper indeed is not the same throughout the surviving manuscripts (though some two dozen of the poems are on the same paper, and this paper appears to be the same as that used for the famous 'Lettre du Voyant' to Paul Demeny of 15 May 1871: *2*, pp.249-54); and it is clear that a shortage of paper at the copying stage — Rimbaud and his cronies were always short of money — led to texts being added in the blanks left at the end of sheets. A change of ink and writing style makes this clear in the case of 'Conte', for example, following 'Enfance' V, and of 'Départ' and 'Royauté' following 'Vies' III. Fénéon therefore used his own judgement (not unreasonably since Rimbaud was believed dead and was actually trading in the Middle East at the time) in adopting an order for the texts, numbering accordingly the sheets that he had before him. Certain groupings, where one poem runs over onto the following sheet, or two or more texts follow each other on the same sheet, imposed themselves, though where a poem has been used to fill in a blank space, even this criterion is highly suspect.

The second complication is that what appeared under the title *Illuminations* in *La Vogue* in four issues of May and June 1886 is both less and more than what is now generally understood by the collection. Less, because five texts, 'Fairy', 'Guerre', 'Génie', 'Jeunesse' and 'Solde' turned up later and were first published in the 1894 edition of the *Poésies complètes*; more, because as well as the prose poems were included not simply 'Marine' and 'Mouvement' which have, rather oddly, been retained with the *Illuminations*, but also eleven verse poems first separated out under the title *Vers nouveaux et chansons* in Paterne Berrichon's 1912 edition of the *Œuvres*. Because the title *Illuminations* has been used to cover different realities, there is a considerable danger of confusion and misunderstanding when reading the early critics, and even now, while the corpus of texts seems agreed, the order of the texts is a matter of choice; as one editor has observed, 'il est clair que toutes ces proses étant sans lien entre elles, leur ordre importe peu, et qu'un classement en vaut un autre' (*4*, p.162). Inertia has therefore become a powerful force in the ordering of the poems, and in this and many other respects what is lacking is any knowledge of Rimbaud's own intentions. Speculation, of course, is rife, but unless and until further documentary evidence comes to light, we are scarcely able to utter more than Verlaine did in 1883, in the very first publication presenting Rimbaud, calling the *Illuminations* 'une série de superbes fragments' (*8*, p.104).

A future editor may well shift 'Marine' and 'Mouvement' to the *Vers nouveaux et chansons*, not simply because, being in free verse, they are indeed 'vers nouveaux' rather than prose poems (among the first, if not the first, *vers libres* in French in fact), but also because of the typography of the poems in the pages of *La Vogue*, which was respected, despite a changed order for the texts in general, in the first edition of the *Illuminations*, prefaced by Verlaine, in 1886 (Publications de *La Vogue*). All the verse poems, unlike the prose poems, were there printed in italics, with the exception of 'Marine', and the reason why 'Marine' appeared in roman type seems to be because, mistakenly, it runs straight into the prose text of 'Fête d'hiver'. 'Les Ponts' was similarly joined on, without a break or title, to 'Ouvriers', but since both are prose poems the particular problem of how to classify one of them does not arise. Berrichon, in his 1912 edition of the *Œuvres* and 1914 edition of the *Illuminations*, separates 'Marine' and 'Mouvement' from the prose texts. He also, on the other hand, in the 1898 edition of the *Œuvres* prepared in conjunction with Rimbaud's schoolfriend Ernest Delahaye, adds to the *Illuminations* one of the texts now habitually grouped separately under the title 'Proses évangéliques' (*2*, pp.162-64).

Careful scrutiny of the manuscripts not only reveals points of detail which have escaped the attention of critics over the past century but has also given rise to, for example, the plausible suggestion that what is printed as 'Phrases' is in fact two distinct sequences, the first three sections divided by lines being one, and the rest (starting 'Une matinée...', after a gap), with its paragraphs (or separate texts?) divided by three crosses, being the other (see *2*, p.989). The most meticulous of younger French Rimbaud scholars, André Guyaux, has suggested a further refinement: because the two parts of 'Phrases' appear on separate sheets, the latter being cut off at top and bottom leaving a cross and a half showing at the bottom, it is not impossible that the brief paragraph printed at the end of 'Being beauteous' and preceded by three crosses, a feature found nowhere else in the collection other than between the second group of 'Phrases', should in fact be attached to 'Phrases' II (as it would be best to call the second sequence), the hypothesis being that it figures where it does solely because there was a gap and paper was at a premium (*43*). If so, all the interpreters who have tried looking for connections between the two paragraphs printed as 'Being beauteous' have wasted their time in the attempt.

A greater waste of intellectual energy has been caused by an issue allowed to occupy far too important a place in Rimbaud criticism: when were the *Illuminations* written? The simple answer at present is that we do not know, even if we were to

agree on what constitutes the collection. And not only do we not
know for the collection as a whole, we do not know for any
single text in it. Not one piece of documentary proof is available
to support the suggestions made on the basis either of internal
evidence (a close and sometimes patently distorted reading of a
given text) or of suppositions from what we know of Rimbaud's
external biography. All too often, this area of ignorance has
exercised such fascination over the minds of scholars and sleuths
that a real analysis of the poetry has gone by the board. A
methodological divide opens, and the biographers and
structuralists make noises at each other across it, hurling
whatever ammunition comes to hand. It is a matter of
consequence at least, and the positions are as firmly as they are
honorably held, the best criticism tending to come from those
who take account of whatever positive ideas and information
come from either party. Less significant, to my mind, because it
does not call into question one's approach to the fundamental
nature of literature, is the squabble as to whether the
Illuminations date from 1871-73, that is to say before *Une saison
en enfer* (dated April-August 1873), or after it, from 1873 until a
date which has varied from 1875 right up until 1879. Since firm
information is lacking, hypotheses are uncontrollable: inter-
pretation must for the time being take account of our ignorance
and make the best of it in pursuit of judicious literary assess-
ments.

Such indirect evidence as exists is confused and often flatly
self-contradictory. Polemical stances have been taken both by
the 'traditionalists', who take *Une saison en enfer* as a farewell
to literature, and the partisans of a reading of that same angry
work as a farewell to a particular kind of (life and) literature.
The publication in 1949 by Henri de Bouillane de Lacoste both
of a critical edition of the *Illuminations* (*4*) and of a celebrated
thesis, *Rimbaud et le problème des 'Illuminations'* (*34*),
triggered off the latter view by 'proving' that the handwriting of
the available manuscripts dated from the period late 1873 to
early 1875. He has the support of one of Verlaine's clearest
pronouncements on the subject, figuring at the beginning of his
preface to the first edition of the *Illuminations*: 'Le livre que

nous offrons au public fut écrit de 1873 à 1875, parmi des voyages tant en Belgique qu'en Angleterre et dans toute l'Allemagne' (*8*, p.107). Other statements in which Verlaine or other friends of Rimbaud suggest an earlier date are systematically set aside, and the problem of dating the composition of a poem from what is accepted as a later copy of it is lightly and confidently dismissed. Charles Chadwick led the attack on the new theory in a closely argued series of papers (*18*), and Bouillane de Lacoste's expertise as a graphologist was roundly challenged by others. Critics now seem to settle, dispassionately resigned to our continuing ignorance of facts in the case, for a period of composition stretching to either side, and even perhaps during, that of *Une saison en enfer*.

Dates continue to be proposed, however, for individual texts, and it is perhaps worth commenting on one or two cases to underline an implied assumption that the critics in question make about Rimbaud's capacities, namely that he has neither memory nor imagination. The reader of the latest biography of Rimbaud is told unequivocally for example that 'Marine' was written during the seven or eight hour overnight crossing from Ostend to Dover which left on Saturday 7 September 1872 (*12*, pp.188-89). No proof is adduced: the internal evidence is apparently sufficient. Yet the internal evidence is specifically ambivalent. There are two major sets of references, one to ploughing the land, the other to ploughing through the sea, either of which could be the vehicle and either the tenor of the sustained metaphor. That ambivalence is not respected by a critic coming unarguingly down on one side; the poem is bisected, trivialised, destroyed. A similarly reductive treatment is accorded to 'Mouvement' by the same critic (*12*, pp.204-5), who informs us that the poem stems from Rimbaud's admiration of the second crossing to England that he made with Verlaine, this time from Antwerp to Harwich on a Great Eastern Railway steamer which left at 4 p.m. on Tuesday, 27 May 1873, and arrived at 6.40 the next morning. Presumably Rimbaud and Verlaine were not the only passengers on board, though they may have been the only 'couple' of their kind, yet there is no suggestion that any of the others, sharing the same experience, produced a poem of the power of 'Mouvement' (see *27*, pp.97-114 for an excellent analysis by Michel Charolles). If one begins to investigate why not, it rapidly becomes clear that the production of poetry has remarkably little to do with anything that would appear in a snapshot, and a great deal to do with an individual's powers of linguistic invention. That memory can store experience is a truism; that the poetic imagination can envision it is amply proved by Rimbaud's great poem of the sea, 'Le Bateau ivre', having been written a full year before he had ever seen the sea. It was Rimbaud himself who wrote: 'Je est un autre' (*2*, p.250), and his poetic identity is indeed distinct from his external biography.

We would be wrong, of course, to ignore established facts of history or biography which may help us to understand the poems more fully, but I for one would rather do without the history than without the poems, however slippery they are to grasp. More telling is information about literary material, since then, by juxtaposition, one sees how Rimbaud reuses and reshapes it. He was a voracious reader, and 'sources' adduced for the *Illuminations* go from the Vulgate to Dante, Plato to Poe, Montaigne to Michelet, Shakespeare to Gautier, Hugo to Flaubert, Captain Cook to *Le Magasin pittoresque*. The real problem of appreciating the *Illuminations* fully, however, is the fact that the sheer variety of the texts demands a continual readjustment of critical focus: each poem, almost, is a new beginning. Anyone who reads a substantial proportion of the editions of the works of Rimbaud, of the three hundred and more books and countless thousands of articles devoted to him, rapidly feels like a gaoler, since at every turn he is offered a new 'key', and his bunch increases in weight, often with useless clutter, all the time. But the fact that keys should so often be felt necessary shows general agreement at least that he remains a fascinating enigma, and this despite Etiemble's exhaustive efforts to discredit and explode the many-sided 'myth' of Rimbaud (*7*). Rimbaud was himself a mythmaker, and enigma and ellipsis are part and parcel of that invention. Other poets have grasped this intuitively and made the appropriate synthesis. Paul Valéry saw it well when he noted in his copy of the first edition of the *Illuminations*: 'Ceci est un cryptogramme d'un genre singulier. Qui saisirait la pensée de l'auteur et la génération du texte irait contre l'intention.' Rimbaud is, in Saint-John Perse's splendidly accurate words of 1913, 'ce poète de l'ellipse et du bond'. Tristan Tzara, for the centenary of Rimbaud's birth, wrote: 'Elle [la poésie] est un perpétuel dépassement, mais celle de Rimbaud, plus précisément, est à l'origine même de cette notion de dépassement qui caractérise la poésie d'aujourd'hui.' René Char: 'Rimbaud le Poète, cela suffit, cela est infini.'

This infinite was generated by an extraordinary young man who abandoned poetry at the age of twenty-one at the latest, and whose main production spans the years 1870-73, that is from when he was fifteen and a half to when he was nineteen. His accomplishment in that time was phenomenal and the speed of his development no less so. Extraordinarily gifted, in 1869 and 1870 he walked off with almost all the top prizes at his school at Charleville, but such dutiful achievements were made largely in response to the sternest of mothers. They did not represent the whole of his being, and the repressed part of him could finally be repressed no longer: the violence of that outburst is still felt in the *Illuminations*. Rimbaud is the volcanic epicentre of his poems, which leave us quaking.

He erupted in various ways, running away from home not once but three times, courting scandal, taking drugs (opium and hashish to our knowledge), satirising established attitudes, indulging in obscenities, letting his hair grow long and then shaving it all off — all the familiar features of an adolescent in revolt against bourgeois society. Only his poetry distinguishes him and makes him worthy of our attention as something more than a usual, if extreme, case of schizoid psychosis: during the few years that his repressed life asserted itself before being dominated in turn by the re-affirmation of bourgeois values, Rimbaud wrote poems.

At first they accepted the traditional mould of verse forms, but in the course of time and under the influence of Verlaine in particular, they explored freer forms. After the sustained *tour de force* of 'Le Bateau ivre', the *Vers nouveaux* show not simply an increased lightness of touch, but also experimentation and success of a high order. The individual forms adopted are chosen not merely for their appropriateness — that would be too decorative a view of their nature — but rather for their organic participation as significant form in the total economy of each poem. This experience in attuning form to purpose and making it participate in that purpose was put to good use in the *Illuminations*, where flexibility of form is total, or potentially so, and can therefore be selected and adjusted by the poet according to his needs, or, more accurately, can grow naturally out of the very totalising collaboration between content and form in the creative process. We shall see in the discussion of particular texts that the form is often controlled, even contrived, in a way unexpected in prose and so all the more invisible and surreptitiously effective.

Just as form is no longer decorative, nor are images. Metaphor is vastly more important here than simile, being precisely the more integrated form. We have already noted how, in 'Marine', vehicle and tenor are indissociable, even indistinguishable. The technique is disorientating, on purpose as we shall see, leaving the reader no clear map of the territory he is exploring, lost in a here and now of the poem's making, able to glimpse only the shifting text in hand by the intermittent light it throws.

How appropriate then the title *Illuminations*! Yet we have seen it qualified by Verlaine by two 'explanatory' sub-titles: 'painted plates' and 'coloured plates', the first of which is clearly unsatisfactory to the English reader, evoking only decorated ornamental china dishes. Since the term 'coloured plates' applies to illustrations in books, the echo of illuminated manuscripts makes this sub-title more acceptable. But do we not now prefer to understand by the title word: sudden inspirations, visions, brilliant insights, as if the title were wholly French? Verlaine's evidence is against it, especially as he gives a pseudo-phonetic transcription of the English pronunciation: '*Illuminécheunes*'. It has been discovered that for an exhibition of Abyssinian manuscripts which Rimbaud saw with his family at the British Museum in 1874, the relevant catalogue title was indeed 'Illuminations'. Rimbaud, on this as on so many other issues, is silent: Verlaine is our sole authority, and he is notoriously unreliable. Yet he alerts us to the central fact that the *Illuminations* are concerned with the visual as well as the verbal, with surfaces, pictures real or imagined, landscapes and events framed, captured in the eternal present of the poems. May the sub-title 'painted plates' not then be a direct echo of Blaise de Vigenère's translation of Philostratus's *Images ou Tableaux de platte peinture* of which copies were available to Rimbaud both at Charleville and at the British Museum? The suggestion has been made with interesting comparisons of the two works by K. Alfons Knauth (*36*). Yet another possible source links the verbal and the visual. Once alerted, the reader is reminded of Baudelaire's art criticism in his 'Salon de 1859', in which the imagination is celebrated as 'la reine des facultés' and its constructive, creative qualities distinguished, as in Coleridge's *Biographia literaria*, from idle fancy, and even more sharply from the photographic copy. Baudelaire is hailed by Rimbaud as 'le premier voyant, roi des poètes, *un vrai Dieu*' (*2*, p.253), and what is particularly significant about this text for the *Illuminations* is that several times the verb 'illuminer' occurs, even underlined on one occasion. It is a faculty of the imagination: 'l'imaginatif dit: "Je veux illuminer les choses avec mon esprit et en projeter le reflet sur les autres esprits"', and Baudelaire's prime example is the painting of Delacroix. There is evidence of Rimbaud's having read the 'Salon de 1859' from verbal echoes occurring in the *Illuminations*, but there seems little doubt that Baudelaire's main distinction between the mere copier of facts and the transformer of those same facts through the creative imagination was a lesson well learnt by Rimbaud, if not by all his commentators.

2. Form

In another way too Rimbaud was indebted to Baudelaire, for his great predecessor had written a volume of prose poems, *Le Spleen de Paris*, published posthumously in 1869. A central question which is put in the preface to the collection seems, in its aims and implied programme, to find a singular response in the *Illuminations*:

> Quel est celui de nous qui n'a pas, dans ses jours d'ambition, rêvé le miracle d'une prose poétique, musicale sans rythme et sans rime, assez souple et assez heurtée pour s'adapter aux mouvements lyriques de l'âme, aux ondulations de la rêverie, aux soubresauts de la conscience?

In the same preface, Baudelaire acknowledges his debt to the very first collection of prose poems, Aloysius Bertrand's *Gaspard de la Nuit*, published posthumously in 1842. The history of the *poème en prose* has been thoroughly traced by Suzanne Bernard (*31*). Dissatisfaction with the way in which verse had atrophied in the eighteenth century, reducing poetry to the merely decorative, was combined with the recognition that prose had been shown, by Rousseau and Chateaubriand in particular, to have a poetic potential ignored or unsuspected before. Where verse was retained, its forms were subjected to new scrutiny and achieved new flexibility, giving rise to a flowering of exquisite and/or robust poetry in the hands of new masters. The prose poem represents a different kind of experiment, and it is one which fundamentally calls into question the traditional assumption that by poetry we mean verse. George Steiner has neatly encapsulated the essential distinction: 'The poetic is an attribute; verse is a technique.'[2] Verse is consequently irrelevant

[2] *The Death of Tragedy*, Faber, 1961, p.238. See also Roger Little, '*Ut pictura*

to poetry, though poetry is not irrelevant to verse. Since the introduction of free verse in the 1870s, with the subsequent variant of the long line of the *verset* (used by Claudel and Saint-John Perse), unrhymed poetry has become not merely familiar but probably the most common form exploited by poets. However, as T.S. Eliot wisely observed, 'only a bad poet could welcome free verse as a liberation from form'.[3] The same is true of the prose poem, but the pressures on shaping it are necessarily different.

Most of the techniques available to the poet in verse are also available to the poet in prose. The principal one which is not is obviously rhyme, but the gain is the capacity, generated by the very flexibility of the medium, to shape the poem on the page in a way inherently appropriate to its subject. It is a feature which will be developed further in the experimental typography of Mallarmé's 'Un coup de dés', Apollinaire's 'calligrammes' and subsequent 'concrete poetry' and work by the Lettrists and Spatialists. The spatial dimension of a poem and the importance of its visual impact are recognised implicitly in the tradition of printing poems with generous margins in which the reader's imagination can in turn go to work: they emphasize the non-linear quality of the text.

I have a theory that the great periods of exploration and achievement in poetic form, the Renaissance and the nineteenth century, are obscurely linked with the major technological leaps in printing at the start of these periods and with the advances in literacy which they heralded. They represent major shifts from an oral community to literate individualism, even isolationism (one reads alone), and with these shifts the visual effect of the printed page takes on, for an increased readership, a new importance. Just as Gutenberg generated fascination for the privileged few — but still for more than a manuscript could reach — and gave rise to experiments in shape and colour by printers and poets, sometimes one and the same person as in the

poesis: an element of order in the adventure of the *poème en prose*', in *Order and Adventure in Post-Romantic French Poetry: essays [for]* ... *C.A. Hackett*, Oxford: Blackwell, 1973, pp.244-56.

[3] 'The Music of Poetry', in *Selected Prose*, Harmondsworth: Penguin, 1953, p.65.

case of Geoffroy Tory, so the industrial revolution marked a further important step:

> The turn of the eighteenth to nineteenth centuries marks a decisive stage in the history of printing. It was not a break but rather a sudden leap forward. It affected the technique of printing, the methods of publication and distribution, and the habit of reading. (...) Technical progress, rationalized organization, and compulsory education interacted upon one another. New inventions lowered the cost of production; mass literacy created further demands, the national and international organization of the trade widened the channels and eased the flow of books from the publishers' stock departments to the retailers' shelves.[4]

Quantity and ephemerality were no doubt encouraged by such new methods, but the poet's fundamental concern with words as objects as well as conveyors of meaning led to his capitalisation on the very fashion of prose.

Whereas Bertrand's prose poems are formally rather timid, reflecting verse-breaks in their even paragraphing, and Baudelaire's show considerable hesitancy between discursive narrative poetic prose and more tightly organised texts,[5] Rimbaud's *Illuminations* are conspicuously successful from this point of view. Not that they reject all reference to prose forms: the title 'Conte' is an obvious case. But by their sheer variety, they alert and retain attention at a high level. It is as if the visual stimulus, real or imagined, enrolled words in the most appropriate expression of its nature.

Several of the poems close in on themselves by rounding off a narrative sequence and offering at or towards the end references which pick up threads from earlier in the text. 'Après le déluge' is a case in point: the disappointment registered at the fresh start offered by the Flood coming to nothing or being rejected is

[4] S.H. Steinberg, *Five Hundred Years of Printing*, Harmondsworth: Penguin, 1966 edition, p.275.

[5] See David Scott's study of *Le Spleen de Paris* in this series, Grant & Cutler, 1983.

epitomised by the negatives used or implied in the last paragraph, and their force is underlined by the shift in verb forms associated with the images of precious stones and flowers. The third paragraph had offered activity and promise:

> Oh! les pierres précieuses qui se cachaient, — les fleurs qui regardaient déjà.

This has slowed for the gems and stopped for the flowers:

> oh les pierres s'enfouissant, et les fleurs ouvertes!

Such repetitions, always with a difference since the second occurrence has the first to relate to, are part of the poet's stock-in-trade. We shall see that other *Illuminations* based on this model have some surprises in store.

Other texts give cumulative lists, whether of colourful performers ('Parade'), features of a city (both 'Villes') or theatres ('Scènes'), fleeting impressions ('Métropolitain'), items to auction ('Solde') or bequeath ('Dévotion'). 'Barbare' combines repetition and listing in a giddy spiral as it both accumulates references ('O Douceurs, ô monde, ô musique' gathers together words used separately before) and uses a refrain to thrust the poem into continued existence after its final *points de suspension* while ironically declaring that what is referred to does not in fact exist.

Other poems are similarly undercut by their closing words, though the eclipse can never, by definition, be total, since the poem continues to exist and haunt us. 'Après le déluge' ends on our ignorance; 'La musique savante manque à notre désir' at the end of 'Conte', the words of the sentence relating in no direct way to words that have gone before; the close of 'Parade': 'J'ai seul la clef de cette parade sauvage' can be variously and perhaps simultaneously interpreted as a proud claim by the poet, as a note of regret at his solitude, and consequently as a challenge or a plea for understanding by the reader; 'Les Ponts' has its intricate design annihilated in a disparaging gesture: '— Un rayon blanc, tombant du haut du ciel, anéantit cette comédie';

midday casts its brash light over the experience recounted in 'Aube', and again the last line: 'Au réveil il était midi', allows of interpretations encompassing disappointment that the vision is lost and an excited recognition of reality in which the experience participates; the closure of 'Nocturne vulgaire': 'Un souffle disperse les limites du foyer', is simultaneously an opening out of the vision and an invitation to re-embark on a reading of the poem, since it starts: 'Un souffle ouvre les brèches opéradiques dans les cloisons'.

Another way in which Rimbaud ends his text on a note of disquieting but exhilarating ambiguity is by leaving his syntax uncompleted through the suppression of a finite verb. Even where a sentence follows, as in 'Being beauteous', it is by no means explanatory. 'Jeunesse' II, sub-titled 'Sonnet', has a last sentence of bewildering complexity, leaving one hanging in mid-air as it were. The last paragraphs of 'Angoisse', 'Métropolitain', the last sentences of 'Ville', 'Ornières', 'Dévotion' lack a main verb, and one is similarly suspended. More usual syntactical ellipses close 'Départ', 'A une raison', 'Fairy', 'Jeunesse'... An intake of breath to cope with an incomplete sentence is held when, unconcluded, it nonetheless comes to an end. However inadequate or inappropriate our self-preparation, we are conscious of that breath held until our mental stutterings begin to organise themselves into a distanced response to the text. It is the hiatus into which the imagination slips to join that of Rimbaud himself, the silence necessary to the vital identity of the poem independent of all other considerations.

That sense of separation is also created by reference to fixed forms. In prose, these are essentially elastic in their length while following certain norms regulating their kind. A tale is recounted in 'Conte', 'Génie' and other texts, a riddle proposed in 'H', and the lists of 'Solde' and 'Dévotion', for example, reflect the stylistic habits of the circumstances evoked: items for sale, a charitable legacy to distribute. The poetry of course goes beyond the fixed form, but we need to remember that the formal support is there. Fixed verse forms also seem to be echoed. Does 'Mystique', for instance, not share many of the features which we associate with a sonnet? The presentation in four paragraphs, the last two separated unusually by a comma rather than a full-stop, invites the comparison. The images of curvature and the carefully balanced itemisation of features to left and right, up and down, underpin the enfolding sense of completeness again appropriate to a sonnet. Furthermore the 'turn': 'Et tandis que...', is a familiar technique in the sonnet where octave and sestet often define their relationship by such devices occurring where the two major divisions of the text meet. Among Rimbaud's verse production, over twenty poems are sonnets, so he had served his apprenticeship in the form. And as if to prove that 'Mystique' is as highly organised as a sonnet, he has worked into his final paragraph a phonetic shape reflecting the curvature of his composition:

> *La douceur fleurie* des étoiles et du ciel et du reste descend en *face* du talus, *comme* un panier, — *contre* notre *face*, et fait l'abîme *fleurant* et bleu *là-dessous.*

The words italicised in my presentation echo each other directly around the pivotal word 'panier', the very curvature of which is thereby emphasised (see *41*). In short, we have here, within a prose sonnet, a kind of palindrome, and it is not the only occurrence in the *Illuminations*. In 'Vies' II, more obviously, the words 'une campagne aigre au ciel sobre' are given a mirror-image a few lines later: 'l'air sobre de cette aigre campagne'. Such reversed repetitions focus attention as a concave mirror concentrates image and light, and act as crucibles for the poet's transformations.

What of the *Illumination* that is actually entitled 'Sonnet' ('Jeunesse' II)? Guyaux has had the text printed with the line-divisions as given by the manuscript (*1*, p.297), and this certainly allows the a-b-b-a rhymes of the first 'quatrain' to be seen clearly, but has the disadvantage of making the text stand out from all the others, especially as it has not been possible to retain the same type-face. (Who knows what subtle effects Rimbaud may have sought in transcribing his other texts?) I have proposed a disposition of the sonnet's fourteen lines which takes

account both of the 'turn' after the octave (here after the word
'Mais') and of the importance of rhyme to a sonnet's form (see
45). By drawing attention to rhyme, one is made more conscious
of the internal rhymes in the text, of its careful rhythmic and
formulaic repetitions, and of the essential fact that this is not a
random piece of prose but one in which semantic and syntactic
difficulties — even incoherence — are set off against a highly
controlled structure of sound pattern. My hypothetical
disposition, with the rhyming syllables italicised (in addition to
the first word, underlined by Rimbaud) is as follows:

Homme de constitution ordinaire, la ch*air*
n'était-elle pas un fruit pendu dans le v*er*g*er*;
— ô journées enfantes! — le corps un trés*or*
à prodiguer; — ô aimer, le péril ou la f*or*ce
de Psyché? La terre avait des versants fert*ile*s
en princes et en artistes, et la descendance
et la race vous poussaient aux crimes et aux deuils:
le monde votre fortune et votre pér*il*.
Mais à présent, ce labeur comblé; toi, tes calculs, — toi, tes
                                                        impati*ences* —
ne sont plus que votre danse et votre voix, non fixées et
                                                        point forc*ées*,
quoique d'un double événement d'invention et de succ*ès*
+ une raison, — en l'humanité fraternelle et discrète par
                                                        l'univers s*ans*
images; — la force et le droit réfléchissent la d*anse*
et la voix à présent seulement appré*ciées*.

The prose presentation allows Rimbaud to create echoes more
easily between groups of words elided in pronunciation and to
cover his tracks by disguising the formal effort. The elisions 'à
prés*ent, ce*' and 'à prés*ent se*ulement', like 'invention' and
'danse', participate, heard but not seen, in the phonetic pattern
of 'impatiences', which seeks a further rhyme and nearly finds
one in the elision of '*sans* images'. It also allows greater mobility
of the rhymes, not necessarily falling on the final syllable of one
of my lines, particularly when a rhyme is supported by

anticipation. Thus 'chair' echoes 'ordinaire' and 'trésor' 'corps', two words before in each case. The lonely sounds of 'descendance' in the 'octave' are amply matched by six echoes in the 'sestet'. The importance attached to sound patterns reminds one of the close link between 'son' and 'sonnet' and reveals again the care which Rimbaud took over composition, so much at odds, apparently, with the extravagance of his subject-matter. Valéry's phrase applied to the *Illuminations*: 'l'incohérence harmonique', is marvellously apt.

In some ways the very fascination that Rimbaud shows with the sound of words at the expense of their meaning is the reason for the semantic non-sequiturs. Carried along, carried away perhaps, by sound, his control of sense seems occasionally to have been abandoned in favour of the irruption of the surprising and the marvellous. A cold analysis of the phrase in 'Métropolitain': 'les atroces fleurs qu'on appellerait cœurs et sœurs, Damas damnant de longueur' recognises the rhyming echoes but is baffled by the lack of logic connecting the elements of the expression. In such instances, there is ample room for the reader's imagination to work, but because it is scarcely given a sense of direction, it never has the satisfaction of achievement, since its responses and movements are insufficiently guided. Where internal rhyme is more judiciously used, however, it can act as a powerful springboard both for the text to advance and for the imagination to leap: 'Elan insensé et infini aux splendeurs invisibles, aux délices insensibles' in 'Solde' catches splendidly in an instance of internal rhyme just the imaginative thrust I have in mind. When towards the end of 'Promontoire', the long sentence seems to be running out of steam, it is lifted by internal rhyme linked with a rhythm which is extended to stretch the reader's capacities and prepare him for the marvellous images which are projected on to the Palace walls: the 'voyageurs' and 'nobles'

permettent, aux heures du jour, à toutes les tarentelles des côtes, — et même aux ritournelles des vallées illustres de l'art, de décorer merveilleusement les façades du Palais-Promontoire.

More succinctly, but no less effectively, the forward thrust of 'Ornières' is effected after a static start reminiscent of 'Mystique' by a series of different devices. First the adjective 'rapides' is attached to 'ornières', reversing the usual sense of ruts by this transfer from the vehicles which made them; then by a clipped *phrase nominale*: 'Défilé de féeries', in which the magical cavalcade is conjured up; finally, the forward drive is given a clear signal by 'En effet' followed by a colon. That colon is like the crack of a whip, and its effect continues throughout the poem.

'Métropolitain' drives relentlessly forward throughout its length, structured by the noun placed after a dash at the end of each paragraph and seemingly encapsulating it. Even the apparently static portrayal of the hermaphrodite faun in 'Antique', drawn perhaps from a pictorial or sculptural representation, is made to dance with all the sensuality appropriate to an evocation of the son of Pan. The creature's body is mobile, turning on the spot for our delectation, just as its name, not mentioned, is revealed by reversing the vowels of a central word in the text: 'cithare' — 'satyre' (see *44*). Even in stillness, there is mobility, and if we can agree with Chadwick that 'les *Illuminations* forment, dans l'ensemble, un ouvrage assez calme et paisible' (*18*, p.96), it is largely by contrast with the highly charged, dynamic but more linear writing of *Une saison en enfer*, for the *Illuminations* too are restless and searching. Contemplation itself seems to generate movement of the objects viewed and trigger off dances and departures in a 'silence atrocement houleux' ('Angoisse'). We shall see later how things come to life, and how Rimbaud is more often caught up in the turning world than capable of reaching its still centre.

Calm and control are often betokened by those texts which round in on themselves, but the form may here be deceptive or ironical. 'Après le déluge' is, as we have seen, a carefully closed text, while 'Départ' is cumulative and open, yet it is apparent that the latter is far calmer than the former. The dialectic of movement and stillness will also command our attention, and the pivotal moments in time and thresholds in space need definition so that we may trace the dynamics of Rimbaud's imagination. Such investigations will inevitably and rightly take us towards the problems of meaning, not one but multiple, while showing that the very form of the poems and of their component elements participates integrally in that meaning and in part determines its effects.

Even details of punctuation make their contribution, and no reader of the *Illuminations* will fail to notice the prominence of the dash. On occasions it follows a comma or a semi-colon and may then, improperly by normal standards, be followed by a capital letter. But the dash is part of the texture, and rather than letting our grammatical hackles rise, we should accept the dynamism afforded by the device.

The evidence presented in this chapter will, I trust, bury once and for all any idea that Rimbaud wrote randomly, however audacious or extreme his adventurous experiences may have been. He left no concerted *ars poetica*, it is true, only scattered comments and the ambiguous visionary programme of the 'Lettres du Voyant' (*2*, pp.248-54).[6] But while each and every *Illumination* has to be treated separately and establish its own criteria for judgement, some sense of pattern emerges in the poetics underlying the writing, and it is an exciting and influential one. Caution is clearly needed in attempting to define that poetics, but if we bear in mind that the texts are our only admissible evidence, it should be possible to work towards a definition. The formal variety apparent in the collection, with evidence of close attention to the shaping of the texts and their parts, with patterns of repetition and reversal, and with the pointed support of phonetics and punctuation, shows Rimbaud in control, with the experience of a Parnassian apprenticeship behind him, even an early mastery in writing Latin verse, yet exploring the medium of prose to powerful effect and capitalising on its flexibility. The important principle of appropriateness seems to govern the form of the *Illuminations*, adumbrated in the 'Lettre du Voyant' to Demeny (*2*, p.252) where the poet is given crucial tasks to perform:

[6] For a fuller commentary on these, see the critical edition of them by Gérald Schaeffer, Geneva: Droz, 1975.

il devra faire sentir, palper, écouter ses inventions; si ce qu'il rapporte de *là-bas* a forme, il donne forme; si c'est informe, il donne de l'informe. Trouver une langue.

3. Movement and Stillness

'Au revoir ici, n'importe où. (...) En avant, route!'
('Démocratie'). The frequently unspecified goals of Rimbaud's
departures seem to increase our sense of his travelling for the
sake of travelling. He was called by Verlaine 'l'homme aux
semelles de vent' and, according to Delahaye and others, was an
inveterate walker, with his native Ardennes as an agreeable
training-ground. His view appears to echo the adage that to
travel hopefully is better than to arrive, and this is again
something he shares with Baudelaire who, in *Le Spleen de Paris*,
not only cries 'Déjà!' after a long sea voyage when others sigh
'Enfin!' with relief, but declares in the text entitled 'Any where
out of the world' (a programme in itself): 'Il me semble que je
serais toujours bien là où je ne suis pas'.

'Mouvement' and 'Métropolitain', both in their titles and
their texts, evoke travelling, the first on board ship and the
second on the underground railway, with an echo of the London
Metropolitan Railway, whose later Paris equivalent is now
known by the familiar abbreviation 'le Métro' (see *11*, *40*).
'Métropolitain' generates enormous momentum right from the
outset: 'Du détroit d'indigo aux mers d'Ossian...' as if a whole
island were crossed with the speed of light, evocations of colour
sweeping the spectrum in the first two lines. The second
paragraph continues the breathless forward rush:

> Du désert de bitume fuient droit en déroute (...) les
> casques, les roues, les barques, les croupes.

By the end one is left dizzy by a number of flashing images
which have conjured up a whole world in their fleeting course:
after the 'mers d'Ossian' we are transported in scarcely qualified
leaps to Samaria and Damascus and thence to 'possessions de
féeriques aristocraties ultra-Rhénanes, Japonaises, Guaranies'

(that is from Germany to the Far East and on to South America) and to the polar ice-cap.

The linear thrust of 'Mouvement' is less strongly emphasised, but the travellers are still 'les conquérants du monde' and the 'bord fuyard' slips rapidly along the 'route hydraulique motrice', this last phrase being, as Nick Osmond recalls, 'a modern version of Pascal's observation: "une rivière est un chemin qui marche"' (6, p.156). Yet that same phrase, by its slight shift from the more usual 'roue hydraulique motrice', the paddles of the steamer, draws our attention to the circular movements implied by the text. 'Le mouvement de lacet' with which the poem opens anticipates the possibility of considering curved movements within the linear progress, and indeed we soon find:

> Les voyageurs entourés des trombes du val
> Et du strom.

Both the waterspouts and the maelstrom evoke circularities by which the travellers are in turn encircled, so the 'Repos et vertige' of line 14 represent the still, vertiginous centre of the vortex. A glance back at 'Métropolitain' shows that full circularity is there only sketched, but that arcs nonetheless appear. The sky itself 'se recourbe, se recule et descend' as if to accompany the train through the tunnel, and when that ordeal is survived (for it has undertones of menace associated with rituals feigning death), 'ce pont de bois, arqué' curves its arch overhead almost as a reconciling rainbow, reminiscent of the one in 'Après le déluge' after the rite of passage of the Flood. The conjunction of the linear and the curved seems to offer a totality of principles for the imagination and are indeed often referred to as masculine and feminine, completing each other in their natural coupling.

'Nocturne vulgaire' exploits that conjunction as part of its text. The horse-drawn vehicle of the poet's journey,

> carrosse dont l'époque est assez indiquée par les glaces
> convexes, les panneaux bombés et les sophas contournés —
> Corbillard de mon sommeil, isolé, maison de berger de ma
> niaiserie,

whose forward movement is conducted by the 'postillon et bêtes de songe' (an attractive revivification of 'bêtes de somme' reminding us that 'somme' means a short sleep as well as a burden, 'songe' deriving from the Latin *somnium* meaning sleep), '*vire* sur le gazon' (my italics) in a turning movement. Its components are curved — 'les glaces convexes, les panneaux bombés et les sophas contournés' — and round things are made rounder as they are seen curling round a flaw in the curved window-pane:

> dans un défaut en haut de la glace de droite tournoient les
> blêmes figures lunaires, feuilles, seins.

The linear movement resumed in the penultimate paragraph is not only hypothetical, continuing the questioning formulations (but without question mark) of the previous two, but the apprehension of it is dismissed by the closing line.

'Vagabonds' unfurls only at the end into a forward motion when the expectation created by the title is realised and a final formula encapsulates the sense of questing urgency which Rimbaud conveys:

> — et nous errions, nourris du vin des cavernes et du biscuit
> de la route, moi pressé de trouver le lieu et la formule.

That same urgency is splendidly enacted in 'Génie', though again intermittently, and only after an evocation in perfect stillness:

> O ses souffles, ses têtes, ses courses; la terrible célérité de
> la perfection des formes et de l'action.
> (...)
> Il nous a connus tous et nous a tous aimés. Sachons,
> cette nuit d'hiver, de cap en cap, du pôle tumultueux au
> château, de la foule à la plage, de regards en regards,
> forces et sentiments las, le héler et le voir, et le renvoyer, et
> sous les marées et au haut des déserts de neige, suivre ses
> vues, ses souffles, son corps, son jour.

While the 'terrible célérité' of the good Genius is followed from one place to another, the writer's attitude remains contemplative, and the text reflects this, and itself, in its closing words by collecting vocables which had previously headed successive paragraphs. The form of the text thus turns back in on itself and counterbalances the headlong chase of the 'Génie'. Early in the text, indeed, Rimbaud makes an important distinction when he refers to 'le charme des lieux fuyants et le délice surhumain des stations'. The considerably greater value attached here to halts reminds us that the *Illuminations* are a work of composed contemplation, even when the dynamism of certain objects is evoked.

Our sense of the mobility of the images depends in part on the extent to which Rimbaud has things move which would normally be fixed. Reversing the habitual and symbolic pattern, water rises in 'Après le déluge': 'Sourds, étang, — (...) Eaux et tristesses, montez et relevez les Déluges'. In 'Enfance' IV, we see 'la jetée partie à la haute mer'. 'La ville (...) nous suivait' ('Ouvriers'); 'des chalets (...) se meuvent sur des rails et des poulies invisibles' ('Villes': 'Ce sont des villes!...') 'des prés de flammes bondissent jusqu'au sommet du mamelon' ('Mystique'); 'l'Allemagne s'échafaude vers les lunes' ('Soir historique'). We also find a 'rêve intense et rapide' ('Veillées') as well as the 'rapides ornières' of 'Ornières' already noted, ruts which in 'Marine' 'filent circulairement vers l'est'. We experience in 'Barbare' a 'virement des gouffres'; in 'Scènes', 'des futaies mouvantes'; in 'Soir historique', 'un ballet des mers et de nuits connues'; in 'Mouvement', 'la célérité de la rampe' (handrail rather than ramp, I should think, despite what several critics imply); in 'Mystique', 'la rumeur tournante et bondissante des conques des mers et des nuits humaines'.

All this activity of objects or concepts not normally mobile gives a busy sense of moving images, but no special priority is given to forward movement, it would seem. Indeed if any pattern emerges as unusually significant, it is curvature or circularity which embraces writer and reader, and the phrase ending 'Marine': 'des tourbillons de lumière', could well stand as an emblem of the collection as a whole.

The nature of that illumination is seen in 'Mystique', where the dynamic curvature suggested by 'tournent', 'mamelon', 'courbe', 'rumeur tournante', 'conques' and, as I have already suggested, 'panier' join the symmetry of reference and syntax, and finally the palindromic form of the last paragraph, in a contemplative focus of considerable penetration. As in 'Métropolitain', the sky curves down, unsullied here by belching smoke, and perfumes and lights up the impenetrable abyss within the poet's mind. The basket acts as a reflector, gathering the light waves into a searing concentration of the vision. It is a superb image of the poem itself, acting as a crucible collecting and distilling material and giving ordinary words a new life in that heady process.

The relationship between movement and stillness changes, as so much else, from text to text, and each rewards scrutiny in this respect. The threshold between action and contemplation is clearly a critical vantage-point, and all the more so when the action is part of the poet's imaginative projection, as is most often the case. For then we step straight into his world at the point of balance and, on the basis of the realities we recognise and grasp, can explore with him the fantastic universe he conjures up. In some respects, our measure of Rimbaud's success in holding his texts in an equilibrium which probes both illusion and reality to an appropriate degree can be assessed by seeing whether the fulcrum is kept in view, whether the poet keeps at least one foot on the threshold.

We have noted the passage through the tunnel in 'Métropolitain' as a rite of passage. It serves as a threshold to a new world, in this case represented by an evocation of the countryside as opposed to the city just left. Its mythological and magical import is hinted at in a series of 'fantasmagories'; 'potages de Samarie', 'masques enluminés', 'ondine niaise', 'crânes lumineux'. Yet still its secret remains hidden: the roads are 'bordées de grilles et de murs' and the inns are forever closed. We travel on, and the secret remains. So does it in a series of closely related images in 'Enfance' II, but there the infinite sadness of a child's weeping makes the high walls and empty inn marvellously moving participants in 'une éternité de chaudes larmes'. Death, absence, emptiness and desolation go hand in hand, the positive elements being restricted to the last paragraph, where the poet imagines himself cradled by a grassy bank, listening to the murmuring of magical flowers and watching fabulous creatures walk round him. We evidently have here a series of symbolic images functioning as projections of the poet's internal drama, and the tension expresses itself in terms of the inner and outer worlds, of loss and gain, of disappointment and escapism. Jean-Pierre Richard rightly sees this as central to our understanding of Rimbaud:

> Le mystère qu'interroge la poésie de Rimbaud, c'est précisément celui de ce passage, de cet avènement du *même* à *l'autre*, celui-là même en vertu duquel la nuit devient aussi du jour, le passé du futur, et le néant de l'être. C'est le mystère de la création.
>
> Voyons donc dans les *Illuminations* un effort, le plus complet peut-être qui ait été tenté par aucun écrivain moderne, pour vivre humainement ce mystère. (*30*, p.193)

What can be judged with some measure of objectivity is whether the imagined barriers which prevent access are successfully converted into frontiers which can be crossed. We have seen how the bounds of the coach in which Rimbaud sees himself in 'Nocturne vulgaire' include a window, and how the very distortions caused by a flaw in the glass participate in the curved enclosing of the womb-like space in which he is carried. The window is there transformed from being a barrier to being a threshold to the rhythmic cycles and security of 'figures lunaires, feuilles, seins'. The window of the poet's snug cottage, 'ma patrie et tout mon cœur', in 'Ville', similarly allows visions of what lies beyond. It is fog! But the fog in turn becomes not a barrier but a frontier, for through it emerge dematerialised figures:

> je vois des spectres nouveaux roulant à travers l'épaisse et éternelle fumée de charbon, — notre ombre des bois, notre nuit d'été! — des Erinyes nouvelles...

Beyond the mediating window, the medium of the fog allows the further mediation of literary echoes — the Furies lurking beyond the entrance to Virgil's hell, the intervention of fairy-folk in human affairs in the wood outside Athens of Shakespeare's *A Midsummer Night's Dream* (a play echoed further in 'Bottom') — to give substance to the vision by relating it to the known.

Jacques Plessen asks: 'ne pourrait-on pas dire que (...) Rimbaud nous relate, dans l'espace spécifique du poème, les aventures — ou les drames — qui arrivent à l'être quand un *dedans* confronte un *dehors*?' (*22*, p.239). In the following forty pages of his book, Plessen explores this confrontation and is led to conclude that 'la poésie de Rimbaud (...) nous montre un être essentiellement frontalier, dont la "dromomanie" [propensity to walk a great deal] peut se décrire comme le mouvement d'un homme qui a perdu son centre' (*22*, p.284). Certainly the hermetic view of a god whose centre is everywhere and his circumference nowhere seems to apply to the elusive, often illusive nature of Rimbaud's work. There are, however, a number of the dramas in the *Illuminations* not simply played out in relation to a perceptible threshold but also using metaphors and references from the theatre (and the related arts of the opera and circus) which allow us to pinpoint that threshold as the frontier between stage and auditorium, between, once again, actor and spectator. But Rimbaud is also the impresario, the director and the stage-manager, and so when we find him perfectly in control of both action and audience there is a strong sense of satisfaction in his accomplishment. If, on the other hand, the balance is not carefully maintained, there is the serious risk of a flop, the twin dangers being an excess either of reality or of illusion. For the fiction of the 'espace pur' of play — in all the multiple senses of the French word 'jeu' — requires, as Roger Caillois points out, 'une conscience spécifique de réalité seconde ou de franche irréalité par rapport à la vie courante'.[7]

Rimbaud's position with respect to play covers the whole possible range. Sometimes he is a spectator, watching developments on stage as if he were quite detached from them. At other times, he is totally caught up in the action. Yet again, he

[7] *Les Jeux et les hommes*, Gallimard, 1958, pp.19, 24.

sometimes straddles the footlights, as it were, joining — and joining in — both the pure space of the vision and the everyday space of the reader/spectator. This mediating stance alone, though not an absolute guarantee of success, allows a kind of poetry to flourish which is both accessible and inspiring. For when Rimbaud is merely a detached spectator, his involvement in the action is passive and prosaic: he is no better placed than the reader of the text to imagine the linking metaphors of illusion and illumination. On the other hand, if he is too exclusively engrossed in his fantasy and in the psychological leaps which he is making, the reader is excluded, able to see only arbitrariness since links are refused. Only by participating in both spaces stretching to either side of the fulcrum, by creating a third term which transcends both reality and illusion, does the poet lead his reader into the marvellous world of his vision. Of course, like the tight-rope walker to whom he likens himself ('Phrases' II), Rimbaud must maintain a delicate balance: one false move brings disaster. Our very sense of the danger is nonetheless important to our appreciation of the daring of the undertaking and of the real achievement on many occasions.

Both 'Ornières' and 'Parade' have been interpreted as circus-parades, and there are features in each which justify this: 'chevaux de cirque' in 'Ornières' and 'tours populaires', 'maîtres jongleurs', perhaps 'comédie magnétique' in 'Parade'. In each case, however, the reader is left to make many imaginative links himself, and while we have seen how effectively dynamic the form of 'Ornières' is, triggered off by the signal of the colon after 'En effet', the very open-endedness of the list that follows is an index of its arbitrariness. The colourful sketch of 'life's rich pattern' is insufficiently developed to retain our attention and commit us to its images other than as a form of words reminding us of childish excitement at such cavalcades. 'Parade', more complex in that it seems to involve not just circus folk but possibly soldiers and 'une cohorte de séminaristes à la promenade' (5, p.97), raises similar problems in that we join Rimbaud as spectators but have the sense of the parade withheld from us. Antoine Adam's interpretation of the poem as a satire of church ritual (2, pp.982-83) incorporating, as various critics have suggested, echoes of Captain Cook's description of pagan ceremonies and the anti-clerical views of the nineteenth-century writers Raabe and Töppfer, is a most interesting reading, but it remains true that the main actors in the parade are presented as fairground characters and may or may not be symbols. We are not given the key to the secret and so remain spectators. There is either too much reality or too much illusion, the novelty and strangeness of the text haunting us perhaps but to little purpose if we cannot participate in a meaning of some, even multiple, kind. Reference to literary influences does not clarify Rimbaud's meaning, but rather shows his assimilation of diverse reading matter in a text made exclusively his own.[8]

It is all the more interesting therefore to find Rimbaud so often associating theatrical references and images of mediation, either spatial or temporal. Bridges, the image of mediation *par excellence*, and the activities around them, are dismissed in 'Les Ponts' as 'cette comédie'. In 'Enfance' III, 'Il y a une troupe de petits comédiens en costumes, aperçus sur la route à travers la lisière du bois'. The edge of the wood is the limit between security and adventure and we share the poet's sense of exhilaration all the more readily because of that threshold. The scene of 'Fleurs', observed from 'un gradin d'or', is the meeting-point of the sea and sky which attract to it a mass of flowers, active and alive as flowers so often are in Rimbaud (capable of speech in 'Aube' and in 'Un cœur sous une soutane' (*2*, p.195)). We share the poet's invention of wonder, and are not fundamentally disconcerted by not knowing whether the theatre is the vehicle or tenor of the structuring metaphor of which the bank of flowers is the other term. As in 'Marine', the balanced tension of that uncertainty is integral to our apprehension of the text. In 'Fleurs' the stage is set at the edge of sea and land, yet another threshold in space, and the whole text focuses on the flower-decked terrace which becomes the crucible of the poet's gaze. A very different structure in 'Scènes', an open-ended list,

[8] Louis Forestier has recently proposed male prostitutes as the 'drôles' tricked out in their tawdry finery: see ' "Parade" ou la parabole', *Berenice* (Rome), 2 (1981), pp.72-76. For a general discussion of the dialectic of the threshold, see my study 'Rimbaud: au seuil de l'illumination', in *26*, n° 2 (1973), pp.81-105.

nonetheless associates theatrical activity and various mediating points of junction: where field meets wood, 'au sommet d'un amphithéâtre couronné par les taillis', at the water's edge, or again, in a final complex meeting-point,

> L'opéra-comique se divise sur notre scène à l'arête d'intersection de dix cloisons dressées de la galerie aux feux.

Perhaps the richest text illustrating this association of a theatrical reference acting as a focal point with images of thresholds is 'Nocturne vulgaire'. The connection made there between forward motion and cradled immobility has already been noted, but that dialectic is engaged only within the broad organisation of the poem, closed in on itself but at the same time thrown marvellously open by the condensed repetition at the end of a sentence divided at the outset:

> Un souffle ouvre des brèches opéradiques dans les cloisons, — brouille le pivotement des toits rongés, — disperse les limites des foyers, — éclipse les croisées.
> (...)
> —Un souffle disperse les limites du foyer.

We thus have a structure and a syntax perfectly formed around a series of images which are purposely disorientating. We find our bearings in part thanks to the dialectic between inside and outside and to the patterns of curvature which have been noted, but we are otherwise allowed to let our imagination set to work. We join the poet in his dream-world, aware of menace ahead — 'les bêtes féroces et les armées', 'les plus suffocantes futaies', 'l'aboi des dogues' — in that essential journey towards 'la source de soie', which is none other than 'la source de soi-même', the softly enveloping matrix of our regressive desire for the absolute protection of the womb. Both danger and security are dispersed by the return to realism of the final line. Yet it is clear that our exploration with the poet of the imagined space before that is made possible by his careful juxtapositions allowing us to share in the awareness of the different thresholds which we have to cross. The first sentence shows us the stage where the drama is to be played out; there follows a journey in which the balance between illusion and reality, interiority and exteriority, is given more importance than the forward motion of the carriage; the unhitching of the horses closes the first paragraph, taking place on a patch of gravel seen as a patch of colour on the window-pane. Thereafter, the dashes, already numerous, launch the paragraphs with new speed, and the questioning mode as well as the static 'Ici' suggests that the journey is now in the mind alone. The horses are stabled in parentheses: their work is done. And whatever interpretation we put on the threats, more or less veiled, of storm, sexuality or spirituality, leading to confrontations with the ocean — 'les eaux clapotantes' — or, microcosmically, 'les boissons répandues', we are aware of a marvellous and perilous journey, envisaged as in 'Le Bateau ivre' where macrocosm and microcosm similarly stimulate the imagination drawn by 'les clapotements furieux des marées' as by 'la flache / Noire et froide' (*2*, pp.66-69). If childish tears can generate such storms, as Marie-Joséphine Whitaker has suggested (cf. *23*, pp.81-87), we are made all the more conscious of the power of Rimbaud's inventiveness. The sense of drama which has breached the bounds of reality is so powerful that its violence wakes the dreamer gazing into the focal centre ('foyer', also meaning hearth and home, as well as the geometrical centres of an ellipse and a theatre foyer) of his very being.

Movement and stillness thus cooperate in various guises to penetrate that being and by their interaction in images of the threshold between them allow us in turn to situate Rimbaud's visions. The insight we gain by that awareness is more essential to our understanding of the poetry than mere comprehension of individual words and phrases.

4. Space and Time

In the last chapter, I emphasised the spatial dimension which provides images of action and contemplation, but it is in fact inseparable from the temporal dimension. A consideration of certain texts including both large and small scale references will show the similarity of Rimbaud's approach to the two dimensions and lead to an appreciation of temporal images of the threshold, no less revealing of the patterns of Rimbaud's psyche than those in space.

'Promontoire' is liberal with its geographical references, whether in the exaggerated comparison with the headland envisaged — 'un promontoire aussi étendu que l'Epire ou le Péloponnèse, ou que la grande île du Japon, ou que l'Arabie!' — or in place-names evoked: 'canaux de Carthage', 'Embankments d'une Venise louche', 'de molles éruptions d'Etnas', 'glaciers', 'peupliers d'Allemagne', 'Arbres du Japon' (plural in the manuscript), Scarbro', Brooklyn, Italy, America, Asia... The use of the plural for singular phenomena (the Embankment in London and Mount Etna) is part of the expansive process of aggrandizement of the modest foreland which begins as no more than 'cette villa et (...) ses dépendances', a rather sumptuous seaside hotel. There is mocking irony in the exaggeration, and the grand classical words 'fanums' and 'théories' for 'temple' and 'procession' respectively bespeak that pretentiousness which Rimbaud is deflating. Even the breeze that wafts across the elegant terraces is rich, partly from 'l'aube d'or' but partly too from its very contact with such luxury and indulgence regardless of cost. The whole world participates in the images which are projected by the poet's imagination on to the palace walls, as if they were those of a universal exhibition conflating contributions from all points of the compass. To reduce all this to a hypothetical visit by Rimbaud to Scarborough, for which there is no external evidence, is to miss the point. A picture of the resort viewed from the sea would have sufficed for the passing reference to Scarbro' in which Rimbaud also shows (off) his knowledge of the pronunciation. What counts is his transformation of an object through disparate allusions, the fragmentation held in check by the clarity of the starting-point. Scarborough has no priority in the hierarchy established by the syntax, egalitarian at that point: 'de Scarbro' *ou* de Brooklyn' (my italics), and nobody has suggested that Rimbaud ever visited Brooklyn.

On a similar large scale but in the temporal dimension is 'Après le déluge'. Striding across time, Rimbaud is often difficult to follow, for the apparent randomness of his references indicate the lack of what would normally be considered the historical sense. His geography, as we have seen and shall see again, is no less random on occasion, and certainly cannot be explained entirely by his nonetheless extensive travels, most of which were undertaken after the completion of both the *Illuminations* and *Une saison en enfer*: 1872, 1873, 1874 Belgium and England; 1875 Germany, Italy; 1876 Austria, Holland, Indonesia; 1877 Scandinavia, Egypt, Italy: 1878 Switzerland, Italy, Egypt; 1878-80 Cyprus; 1880-91 Aden, Ethiopia... In 'Après le déluge', pell mell, we find the Flood, Bluebeard, Eucharis (a character from Fénelon's *Télémaque*), a 'Splendide Hôtel', a piano, and 'mazagrans', coffee laced with spirit, drunk in stemmed china beakers now known by the same name after the battle of Mazagran in Algeria in 1840 when General Lelièvre — wittily reduced here to 'Un lièvre' perhaps — distinguished himself. (The hamlet of Mazagran some 10 kms south of Madame Rimbaud's family home at Roche, where *Une saison en enfer* was written, seems also to owe its name to that battle.) We are therefore forced to interpret, and to take some if not all of such references as symbolic. They exist conjointly only in the text of the poem which in turn reflects the present time of the poet's mind at the moment of writing. The most plausible interpretation of the poem as Rimbaud's excitement at — and subsequent disappointment at the failure of — a social revolution, is therefore highly ironic, in that it would show him to have an acute sense of contemporary history. Either we accept this paradox and see Rimbaud as endowed with a political sense but unable to find adequate formulations for it (the view taken by Osmond: see *6*, pp.48-49), or we see him rather as purposely shuffling the cards so as to create an effect which makes the past, the whole past, represented by a variety of datable allusions, participate in the present of the poem. I have a firm belief in the latter view, but it is not impossible that both views are correct, Rimbaud's poetry always seeming to demand a 'both/and' response rather than an 'either/or' one, in this being like all great poetry and unlike the tendency of criticism.

At the more intimate and immediate end of the scale stands, for example, 'Enfance' V, as a representation of an enclosed space, in this case deep underground. It is seen as a tomb, a 'salon souterrain', far below the level of the sewers and the city, with the thickness of the globe for walls, and a wan 'apparence de soupirail' high up by the ceiling the only link with the world above. Or rather the only visible link, since the poet's mind can conjure up infinite space: 'nuit sans fin', 'les gouffres d'azur, des puits de feu', 'lunes et comètes, mers et fables'. And although the rejection of the city is manifest, it has to be mentioned as a foil for Rimbaud's acceptance of his subterranean vault and prompting of our approval. 'Je suis maître du silence' assumes a positive character because of the dialectic pursued; otherwise it might appear to be a gratuitous paradox on the lips of a poet.

A direct comparison may be made with the starting-point of 'Vies' III:

> Dans un grenier où je fus enfermé à douze ans j'ai connu
> le monde, j'ai illustré la comédie humaine. Dans un cellier
> j'ai appris l'histoire.

Gradually, however, as one situation succeeds another, there is expansion. After the attic and the cellar comes 'quelque fête de nuit', then 'un vieux passage' and finally 'une magnifique demeure cernée par l'Orient entier'. The recurrent dream of increasing space and power sends the poet rocketing to a point where to say 'Je suis réellement d'outre-tombe' has meaning as a statement of having gone beyond mundane experience. 'Décidé-ment, nous sommes hors du monde' declares Rimbaud in *Une saison en enfer* (2, p.101), and one way of being out of the air, as Hamlet observed, is to be in the grave: 'C'est un tombeau, je m'en vais aux vers, horreur de l'horreur!' (ibid.). If that is the tomb/womb of 'Enfance' V, it may well be that we should endow the dismissive word 'cela' of 'Vies' III — 'Il ne faut même plus songer à cela' — with all the distaste of an episode scarcely mentionable and best forgotten, a kind of death. With the return to a sense of duty, that distaste may amount to disgust if commentators are right, and I suspect they are, in linking 'cela' with the experiences of drugs and sex shared with Verlaine and recounted in 'La Nuit de l'enfer' (2, pp.99-102) and generally in *Une saison en enfer*. There is, however, a less immediate and tangible sense in which the idea of the existing world gives way to insights beyond its surfaces. The 'possibilités harmoniques et architecturales' ('Jeunesse' IV) which lead the poet on are part of his ambition for poetry, and a high aim bound both to bring failure and simultaneously to make these failures relative.

The privileged moments of vision, often dismissed disparagingly at the ends of texts as we have seen, lest the poet's vulnerability be assailed, may be those describing a scene, taking only so long as one needs to read the words, or recounting a series of events which add up to a crucial experience, or again hovering between the two. In the first category one finds 'Les Ponts', for instance, presented from the outset in pictorial terms: 'ciels' (the plural which tends to be reserved for painted skyscapes) and 'dessin'. As always, the picture is brought to life, here with touches of colour and strains of appropriate music appearing before the image is erased by a shaft of light, a shaft of Rimbaud's self-deflating irony. 'Mystique', hovering uncertainly in the reader's mind between being a description of a picture infused with life and being a transfiguration of some observed reality, has no final deflation. It captures a marvellous moment of insight and warms with all the inspiriting warmth of the hieratical angels-cum-sheep in their woollen coats. The sense of the starry sky brushing balmily past our faces on its way towards the depths brings a thrill of total inclusion in the vision.

'Aube' falls rather in the second category, following a narrative sequence ending in the last sentence returning poet and reader to the light of common day (see *15*, pp.68-73 for an excellent commentary by C.A. Hackett). In a letter to Delahaye (*2*, p.266), Rimbaud called dawn 'cette heure indicible, première du matin'. The word 'aube', it will be recalled, is the period before 'l'aurore', daybreak. The quality of its light and the stillness of the hour are both important to Rimbaud's poem. The extravagant claim made at the beginning leads to an account of how he achieved the embrace of dawn, and part of his secret is that dawn is personified as a goddess. As master of silence, now in a most positive sense, he has the power to waken 'les haleines vives et tièdes' of creatures in the forest, to exchange glances with precious stones, to hear the flowers speak (as he hears them 'mugir' in 'Villes' ('Ce sont des villes!...')). He climbs towards a waterfall as the light increases: the 'frais et blêmes éclats' give way to the 'wasserfall blond' and then to the 'cime argentée'. This is the highest point reached in the poem: from now on the chase is downhill and across the plain, and having seen Rimbaud's careful organisation of other poetic structures, it is of note that he should situate this high point at the very centre of his text, in the fourth paragraph of seven, in line ten out of twenty in many editions. As dawn is chased away by the appearing of the sun over the horizon, so the poet pursues his allegory, as if where the sunlight had not yet penetrated — in the shadow of belfries and domes, in a dark laurel wood — dawn could still be found. The embrace so long desired is realised, if at all, in the last pocket of shade at the foot of the wood, and despite the removal of veils, sufficient remain for discretion, so that the precise nature and extent of the embrace is not revealed. But that something as vast as dawn should be enfolded so intimately in the compass of the poem, as if by the first and last lines, is in itself an extraordinary poetic achievement, and the final unsentimental octosyllabic statement harks back to the opening octosyllable, echoing its phonetic pattern closely to give a sense of absolute completeness.

The satisfaction is increased by our awareness of dawn being the threshold of day, and of the delicate balance enacted in the form of the poem, the balance between dawn and sunrise. Rimbaud sees the poet as the 'fils du Soleil' and 'voleur de feu' bringing illumination and Promethean fire (cf. 'Vagabonds' and the 'Lettre du Voyant', *2*, p.252). Apollo the sun-god is present in 'Aube' in various ways: in the bringing of light, in the myth of his pursuit of Daphne who, to escape from him, was transformed into a laurel tree, and in his role as the god of lyric poetry. Laurel leaves crown both a victor and a poet, and if the laurel wood of 'Aube' remains an ambiguous symbol it is because the extent of the poet's conquest is not revealed. That it might have a mythological explanation is suggested by a consideration of the poem in the light of Max Müller's account recorded in the following passage by Ernst Cassirer:

> Or take the myth of Daphne, who is saved from Apollo's embraces by the fact that her mother, the Earth, transforms her into a laurel tree. Again it is only the history of language that can make this myth 'comprehensible', and give it any sort of sense. Who was Daphne? In order to answer this question we must resort to etymology, that is to say, we must investigate the history of the word. 'Daphne' can be traced back to the Sanskrit *Ahanâ*, and *Ahanâ* means in Sanskrit the redness of dawn. As soon as we know this, the whole matter becomes clear. The story of Phoebus and Daphne is nothing but a description of what one may observe every day: first, the appearance of the dawnlight in the eastern sky, then the rising of the sun-god who hastens after his bride, then the gradual fading of the red dawn at the touch of the fiery rays, and finally its death or disappearance in the bosom of Mother Earth.[9]

Either Rimbaud knew some version of this account or he

[9] *Language and Myth*, New York: Dover, 1953, p.4. The power of creation through language functions in a similar way in Judaeo-Christian mythology, as when Adam was created from the 'dust of the earth' (*adamah* in Hebrew) and woman (*ishshah*) as an extension of man (*ish*). For a different 'Lecture mythique d'"Aube"', see Marc Eigeldinger in *29*, pp.141-51.

instinctively recreated the myth and linked the idea of dawn with the idea implicit in his reference to the laurel tree. Disappointment seems written into the last line of Rimbaud's poem, yet the return to banality is also a contrast with what has preceded, and a touch of irony is possible if we consider that Rimbaud is standing masterfully on the threshold between the ordinary world of his reader, represented by the closing line, and the ecstatic world of his vision which he enters with such consummate aplomb in the first. If there is any sense of catastrophe in 'Aube', as has been suggested, it is essentially in the etymological sense of that word alone: a turning fall, a tumble from the summit to the shady foot of the wooded hill, for any disappointment implied in the text is redeemed by the power of the evocation and by the quality of its totally appropriate structure. The magic surrounding the poet's progress through the forest continues, because he is master of it, to work in his favour.

Is Rimbaud also master of the historical past and specifically of his own past? The answer seems complex, but a distinction emerges between 'enfance' and 'jeunesse' to which Osmond, for example, attributes different values (6, p.34), 'force' being 'a positive presence at the heart of "jeunesse"' but absent from 'enfance'. Clearly it would be wrong to limit the sense of those terms, especially when they are used as titles without an article, as is so often the case with titles in the *Illuminations*, to Rimbaud's own life. They cannot but be based on personal experience, but personal experience always includes the observation of other people and in this case takes on the visionary mantle, so that 'enfance' and 'jeunesse' become also symbolic generalities. One feature of the distinction between them, perhaps because 'jeunesse' is so much less distanced in time from the moment of composition, is that 'enfance' alone seems able to assume the role of threshold. It is not simply more sharply delineated: it appears capable of fulfilling a mediating function in the elaboration of the poet's vision and is in turn linked with many spatial images of the threshold. It is as if 'enfance' corresponded to 'aube' and 'jeunesse' to 'aurore' on a greater time scale.

In 'Enfance' for example, there is a multiplicity of images of mediation: the idol is one at the start, as are the beaches which are its 'domaine'; the scene changes to the edge of a forest, to 'les terrasses voisines de la mer' and is eclipsed at the end of the first section by a derisive dismissal of small-talk by the colourful and statuesque procession which had previously been evoked in grand terms. The association of death and absence with various references to partitions and points of juncture in 'Enfance' II, already noted, culminates in an evocation of calvaries (the Christian image of mediation *par excellence*) immediately undercut in the dispersion of 'les moulins du désert, les îles et les meules', where the echo of 'moulins' in 'meules' seems to have usurped the semantic function (as 'écluse' is prompted by 'enclume' in the same paragraph) and left only a broadcasting of images, or a kaleidoscope as Delahaye called it (*9*, p.86), for the reader to attempt to pattern into sense. The disorientation continues in the syntactically unprepared and unexplained '*le*' of 'Les talus *le* berçaient.' (The word is underlined in the ink of the manuscript and should consequently be printed in italics as it is by Guyaux alone: see *1*, p.256.) Yet we are given so many clues to the atmosphere of desolation that we readily imagine a child bewildered by the impenetrability of the adult world, consoled only by escape into communion with nature and his own imaginings, and seeing his floods of tears as a veritable ocean. The shift of tense, however, from the staccato present of the first three paragraphs to the imperfect recollection of the last, suggests a controlled shift of viewpoint by the poet, and the fact that 'Enfance' III moves to the immediate but also absolute present of 'il y a' further prompts the reader to see the poem as a group of carefully articulated parts. For the present of the first and second sections is a kind of historic present, distanced precisely by the imperfect tense at the end of part II. The present of the last two sections is more genuinely present, leaning into the future towards the close of part IV — 'Je serais...', 'en avançant' — and reaching the wishful thinking of the last paragraph of part V. The last sentence is Rimbaud's usual corrective: after 'je m'imagine...' and the claim 'Je suis maître du silence', the cold light through the basement window casts doubt on the validity of such arrogance, gently mocking.

This relationship between time and tense suggests that while experience nuances or goes so far as to ridicule the absolutes of childhood, the validity of those absolutes is not entirely lost. Like the statements in 'Enfance' III, they stand jewel-like and simply are. Adult explanations are irrelevant, adult logic has no purchase. They have the quality of dreams, where the narrative links of comprehensibility are suppressed and the reader like the poet must stretch his tight-rope from star to star.

'Enfance' realises this vision and allows us to penetrate it, for its concrete allusions remain unexplained yet we share the poet's pivotal position and accept the specificities juxtaposed. The same does not seem to be true of 'Jeunesse', where not only is the reader excluded by obscurity but the tendency is towards abstractions. In 'Mystique', the sky actually descends; in 'Jeunesse' I, we read of 'l'inévitable descente du ciel'. It is a shift from vision to explanation. The sentence 'De petits enfants étouffent des malédictions le long des rivières' seems to summarise the last paragraph of 'Enfance' II, to explain its contents. The splendid statements at the close of 'Jeunesse' IV are eminently quotable as fragments of Rimbaud's poetics, but by their very abstraction are less than satisfactory as poetry:

> Ta mémoire et tes sens ne seront que la nourriture de ton impulsion créatrice. Quant au monde, quand tu sortiras, que sera-t-il devenu? En tout cas, rien des apparences actuelles.

It is precisely those 'apparences actuelles' which nourish Rimbaud's poetry, and for him to refuse them is to refuse the very basis for shared access to the world of his visions. The power of poetic evocation might almost be considered to be in inverse proportion to logical demonstration. This does not imply abandonment of reality but its transformation by the intuitive imagination and the power of words.

When Rimbaud's imagination engages with the history of his time and with the external manifestations of what for him was the latest technology, there are some impressive instances of that engagement in the *Illuminations*. Other critics have evoked some general trends of the era reflected in Rimbaud's work, or noted the influence upon him of Michelet's synthesising writings on broad tracts of history. Let one stand for many:

> Dans les années qui précèdent 1870 toute une littérature révolutionnaire annonçait pêle-mêle des bouleversements cosmiques, l'émancipation de la femme, la fin de toutes les servitudes, de celle même de l'homme en face des lois du monde matériel. Rimbaud s'est formé dans cette atmosphère d'illuminisme social.[10]

True in general terms, this statement is vitiated by a cause-and-effect relationship affirmed in the sentence which precedes it: 'Si Rimbaud a voulu être le Voyant, c'est parce que depuis cinquante ans toute une tradition de pensée liait la cause du progrès social à celle d'une révolution métaphysique.' Rimbaud himself seems congenitally incapable of making that link. However active he may have been as a visionary on the one hand and as a socio-political agitator on the other (and the evidence is fragmentary on both counts), the two were never really pulled together into focus (cf. *6*, pp.48-49). The very nature of his poetic revolution subsumed all other realities: by definition, it was all or nothing for Rimbaud, and his abandonment of creative writing after *Une saison en enfer* and the *Illuminations* appears to be his own intuitive recognition of this.

He did also revert, however, to bourgeois capitalism, whereas there is evidence within the *Illuminations* that the idea of 'la nouvelle harmonie' ('Angoisse') includes a vision of a changed social order. Is it as poetry, however, or as political comment that the wishful thinking: 'Un pas de toi, c'est la levée des nouveaux hommes et leur en-marche' ('Angoisse') is less satisfactory than, say, the surges of excitement and disappointment in 'Après le déluge'? The very question seems wrong just because political thoughts are data of the poems in exactly the same way as any other data. If the poems are successful as

[10] Antoine Adam, 'L'Enigme des *Illuminations*', *Revue des sciences humaines*, 60 (oct.-déc. 1950), p.244.

poems, they will bear with them the marks of an adolescent's proper dissatisfaction with the status quo; if we read them as tracts, we shall be given no new political insights and we shall miss the poetry. Rimbaud's sense of time includes but goes infinitely, if fitfully, beyond his awareness of the contemporary. It is not for maturely considered reflections that one reads Rimbaud, but for the sporadic stimulus of his wayward, youthful genius.

How one understands then his excitement at travelling on the first underground railway, and at discovering the great cities of Paris and London with their bustle and enormous public buildings. For one whose scale was established by the Place Ducale at Charleville, the technical wizardry and sheer size of the Albert Hall or the Crystal Palace could not fail to be impressive. History and place come together in Rimbaud's urban poems, but it would be as wrong-headed to try and situate them exclusively as reactions to particular buildings or events as it would be to try and use them as a guide-book. These are cities of the mind, and although there seems every reason to recognise responses to London in 'Ville', it is the responses that interest us, not the city. Historians confusing literature with life will protest, for example, that the absence of 'les traces d'aucun monument de superstition' is inaccurate as regards London. What is of more consequence is the sequence of negative presentations, actual or implied. Even the narrator cannot bring himself to admit to being more than 'point trop mécontent'. 'Tout goût connu a été éludé', 'vous ne signaleriez', 'réduites', 'n'ont pas besoin', 'plusieurs fois moins long', 'spectres', 'la Mort sans pleurs', 'un Amour désespéré': each sentence contains one or more negative charges, depriving each referent of substance, each body of flesh and life. The three stages of life — 'l'éducation, le métier et la vieillesse' — seem reflected in the latter-day Furies symbolised by Death, Love and Crime. We are as much in the insistent ghastliness of a Dickensian East End or Coketown (in *Hard Times*, which we know Rimbaud read in translation: see *9*, p.80 and *15*, p.150, n.17) as in a real town. Whether the inspiration be reality or a literary expression of that reality, the quality of the result depends on literary techniques of transformation. From the relatively light beginning the image darkens and a new hell circumscribes us, the one salvation residing tenuously in the first adjective of the text: 'éphémère', which simultaneously promises an escape and betokens the permanence of the social and physical hell of the city. As Rimbaud observes in 'Ouvriers', 'la ville, avec sa fumée et ses bruits de métiers, nous suivait très loin dans les chemins', a process which is actualised in 'Métropolitain'. The city is a world apart, but invasive, and when there, the poet longs for 'l'autre monde, l'habitation bénie par le ciel et les ombrages'.

That longing is expressed in quite different ways in the two texts entitled 'Villes', which I shall refer to by their opening words. In 'Ce sont des villes!...', the oneiric conglomerate tends to stress the past in the vision of the present, whilst in 'L'acropole...', the emphasis is almost exclusively on the spatial. Both texts have not unreasonably been taken as reactions to London, then pulsating heart of a world-wide Empire which made it the cosmopolitan centre of extraordinary vitality and diversity which, even with the dismantling of colonialism of that brand, it has remained. The references to London in 'L'acropole...' put the reader on his guard, however, against a simplistic equation. Hampton Court and London are mentioned, but as points of comparison only: 'des locaux vingt fois *plus* vastes *qu*'Hampton-Court', 'quelques nababs *aussi* rares *que* les promeneurs d'un matin de dimanche à Londres' (my italics). The same is true of a reference to Paris, while the Sainte-Chapelle of that city, a building of the high gothic style, is made unrecognisable by being given a huge dome. Even if the term 'Sainte-Chapelle' has been transferred by Rimbaud to, say, the Crystal Palace, the diameter of some fifteen hundred feet is an exaggeration which continues the chain of hyperboles which are, as it were, the 'armature d'acier artistique' of the text. From the outset, we are invited to imagine architecture on a vast scale almost defying conceptualisation. Phrases pile up to this effect: 'les plus colossales', 'Impossible d'exprimer', 'un goût d'énormité singulier', 'vingt fois plus vastes', 'colosses', 'candélabres géants', 'quinze mille pieds de diamètre', 'prodige', 'la reconnaissance est impossible', 'huit cent[s] à huit mille roupies' (the s of 'cents' is missing in the manuscript copied by Germain Nouveau), 'je renonce à me faire une idée', 'qui remplit l'occident éternel'. To such direct mind-boggling expansiveness are added supportive references, ranging widely, the most notable of which are those to human beings who combine an element of the foreign and fabulous with an element of reality: 'Un Nabuchodonosor norwégien', 'subalternes (...) Brahmas', 'quelques nababs', 'gentilshommes sauvages'. We should not be tempted into stressing the real at the expense of the fabulous; indeed in such conjunctions reality must of necessity yield to the imagination's power of subversion.

In 'Ce sont des villes!...', the dream-world we enter is specifically alluded to at the beginning and end of the text, so that we know where we stand. 'Ces Alleghanys et ces Libans de rêve' give the scale and announce the unreality; and at the end, the regretful withdrawal from the dream is equally clear:

> Quels bons bras, quelle belle heure me rendront cette région d'où viennent mes sommeils et mes moindres mouvements?

Within the dream, the temporal dimension is markedly stressed by reference to figures from history and mythology. Some are evoked directly: 'les Rolands sonnent leur bravoure' echoes the famous horn-call recorded in *La Chanson de Roland*, the plural form suggesting a generalisation of heroic last stands. 'La naissance éternelle de Vénus' likewise stresses that it is not a single occurrence but, in the very nature of myth, constantly repeated. 'Des cortèges de Mabs' seem to have escaped from Mercutio's speech in *Romeo and Juliet* (act I, scene iv), and the goddess Diana from her legends. Myth is brought vividly up to date: we find 'les Bacchantes' in the suburbs and Venus at the blacksmith's. In short: 'Toutes les légendes évoluent et les élans se ruent dans les bourgs.' It is an important function of myth that it be reinterpreted and rediscovered afresh by each generation and indeed by each artist: harbouring eternal truths about the human condition both individual and collective, it is here brought alive again for the modern sensibility. The very fact that Roland, Queen Mab, Diana and Venus are known through earlier works of literature or painting — and to them may be added 'des corporations de chanteurs géants' borrowed in all probability from Wagner's *Meistersinger* — is a reminder of the perpetual validity of the archetypes, and Rimbaud's interpretation is splendidly applicable to the industrial urban era. As he declares in *Une saison en enfer*: 'Il faut être absolument moderne' (*2*, p.116). Time dilates from the immediate moment to encompass the dimensions of history and myth in his highly personal vision.

The difficulties of the task of being absolutely modern for Rimbaud's vacillating sensibility are apparent from certain epithets he associates with reality:

> Moi! moi qui me suis dit mage ou ange, dispensé de toute morale, je suis rendu au sol, avec un devoir à chercher, et la réalité rugueuse à éteindre! (*2*, p.116)

'Bottom' begins: 'La réalité étant trop épineuse pour mon grand caractère,' and the poet is soon indulging in fantasy and escapism, transformed in succession into a blue-bird, a bearskin rug, a fish (implicitly in the third paragraph perhaps), an ass braying for the attention of the 'Sabines de la banlieue', close cousins of the 'Bacchantes des banlieues' of 'Ce sont des villes!...'. Frustration is prompted not only by the city: it also appears here to be of a sexual order. It is the rape of the Sabine women which history and art have most remembered and consecrated, and Rimbaud's fluctuations between involvement and rejection, between immersion and extraction, between ecstasy and disgust operate at many levels. Some of the more private, indulged when he felt 'dispensé de toute morale', need investigation.

5. The Unspeakable and the Ineffable

In order to grasp something of the thinking behind the *Illuminations*, two other texts by Rimbaud are essential reading: the principal 'Lettre du Voyant', as it is known, which Rimbaud sent to Paul Demeny on 15 May 1871 (*2*, pp.249-54) and *Une saison en enfer* of 1873 (*2*, pp.91-117). The precise relationship between either of them and the *Illuminations* is uncertain, but reflection on certain passages undoubtedly guides the reader towards a better understanding of Rimbaud's general approach to poetry around the time he wrote his prose poems.

The 'Lettre du Voyant' is so called because of a key passage of central interest to the *Illuminations*:

> Je dis qu'il faut être *voyant*, se faire *voyant*.
> Le Poète se fait *voyant* par un long, immense et raisonné *dérèglement* de *tous les sens*. Toutes les formes d'amour, de souffrance, de folie; il cherche lui-même, il épuise en lui tous les poisons, pour n'en garder que les quintessences. Ineffable torture où il a besoin de toute la foi, de toute la force surhumaine, où il devient entre tous le grand malade, le grand criminel, le grand maudit, — et le suprême Savant! — Car il arrive à l'*inconnu!*

Every writer on Rimbaud has had to come to terms with the implications of this text, with the variety of ways in which the poet turns himself into a visionary, including some which appear contradictory. If '*dérèglement*' is stressed, it is nevertheless 'raisonné'; '*tous les sens*' may be interpreted as representing two distinct stages of the creative process, relating either to the perceptions of the senses or to all the senses of the words selected for the poems. By 'il épuise en lui tous les poisons', do we understand that he absorbs them or expels them in order to reduce them, one way or the other, to their quintessence? How should we reconcile the characteristics that Rimbaud attributes to the visionary: 'malade', 'criminel', 'maudit', 'Savant'? We must ourselves stretch our imaginations to encompass these diverse concepts and attune our senses to the 'ineffable torture' claimed as necessary to the penetration beyond the threshold of the unknown.

Baudelaire had expressed his sense of that ineffable torture when addressing Death in the last verse of the last poem of *Les Fleurs du mal*, 'Le Voyage':

Verse-nous ton poison pour qu'il nous réconforte!
Nous voulons, tant ce feu nous brûle le cerveau,
Plonger au fond du gouffre, Enfer ou Ciel, qu'importe?
Au fond de l'Inconnu pour trouver du *nouveau*!

Baudelaire, seen by Rimbaud as 'le premier voyant', spent his poetic life attempting vainly to escape from the menace and grip of 'l'Ennui', a metaphysical spleen that haunts his work and being, and in one of his prose poems, 'Enivrez-vous', he suggests drink, poetry and virtue as interchangeable means of at least temporary relief, insisting on the necessity of intoxication by any means:

Il faut être toujours ivre. Tout est là: c'est l'unique question. Pour ne pas sentir l'horrible fardeau de Temps qui brise vos épaules et vous penche vers la terre, il faut vous enivrer sans trêve.
Mais de quoi? De vin, de poésie ou de vertu, à votre guise. Mais enivrez-vous.

In *Les Fleurs du mal*, he adds the expedient of sex to the drugs (represented here by wine, but elsewhere in his work by opium and hashish) and to the headiness engendered by poetry and the practice of virtue.

Rimbaud seems to have been little attracted to the last during the rebellious stage of his life. His experiments were as calculated but more perverse. That his 'poison' was hallucinogenic is suggested in this passage from *Une saison en enfer*:

> Je m'habituai à l'hallucination simple: je voyais très-franchement une mosquée à la place d'une usine, une école de tambours faite par des anges, des calèches sur les routes du ciel, un salon au fond d'un lac; les monstres, les mystères; un titre de vaudeville dressait des épouvantes devant moi.
> Puis j'expliquai mes sophismes magiques avec l'hallucination des mots! (*2*, p.108)

The difficulty one has in following some of the notations in the *Illuminations* derives in part from this double hallucination, first distorting sense-perceptions and then applied consciously to words, and so encapsulating the double meaning of '*tous les sens*'. The pattern of oneiric engagement followed by final withdrawal — with the accompanying symptoms of disorientation — which we observe in so many of the *Illuminations* mirrors the effects of certain drugs. The experiences of hallucinogens recorded by the twentieth-century poet Henri Michaux are often referred to as authoritative, and indeed his expression of his visions often resembles Rimbaud's. Among nineteenth-century writings on the subject, Rimbaud had certainly read Baudelaire's *Paradis artificiels*. A passage from Nerval's *Voyage en Orient* (quoted by Bonnefoy, *13*, p.164), another work which Rimbaud almost certainly knew, describes effects of direct interest to readers of the *Illuminations*:

> Le haschisch rend pareil à Dieu. (...) L'ivresse, en troublant les yeux du corps, éclaircit ceux de l'âme; l'esprit, dégagé du corps, son pesant geôlier, s'enfuit comme un prisonnier dont le gardien s'est endormi, laissant la clef à la porte du cachot. Il erre joyeux et libre dans l'espace et la lumière, causant familièrement avec les génies qu'il rencontre et qui l'éblouissent de révélations soudaines et charmantes. Il traverse d'un coup d'aile facile des atmosphères de bonheur indicible, et cela dans l'espace d'une minute qui semble éternelle, tant ses sensations s'y

succèdent avec rapidité.

The return to reality is of course less pleasurable.

It is impossible to ascertain which, if any, of the texts in the *Illuminations* are directly provoked by drug-taking, which model themselves on such experiences and which create similar illusions without any reference to drugs. Suggested as possible candidates for recording an experience with hashish have been 'Antique', 'Being beauteous', 'Nocturne vulgaire', 'Angoisse', 'Barbare' and 'Génie'. The poem most widely accepted as being in this category, however, is 'Matinée d'ivresse'. Implied by the title, the fact seems clinched by the final word *'Assassins'*, the etymology of which is to be found in the Hashishins. Baudelaire, in 'Le Poème du haschisch' in his *Paradis artificiels*, equates hashish with *cannabis indica*, Indian hemp, and recounts that when it is harvested, 'la tête du moissonneur est pleine de tourbillons, quelquefois chargée de rêveries' (chapter 2). Rimbaud too, in a deleted sentence of his draft for *Une saison en enfer*, records the feeling: 'Les hallucinations tourbillonnaient trop' (*2*, p.170), and this spiralling, whirling effect is present in the structure both of 'Matinée d'ivresse' and of 'Barbare' as well as in several other texts by reference or implication. Indeed one of Rimbaud's claims in *Une saison en enfer* is: 'Je fixais des vertiges' (*2*, p.106). The very control in the verbal 'fixing' of delirium, the very shaping of the texts through repetition, obliges us however to acknowledge the work of the poet and to recognise the essential difference between the experience in itself and the emotion recollected in turmoil.

The initial personalisation of the universals 'Bien' and 'Beau' in 'Matinée d'ivresse' seems to indicate opposite possibilities: on the one hand a fragment of each is claimed as Rimbaud's own (the subjective sense used by Baudelaire in his *Journaux intimes: Fusées*, X: 'J'ai trouvé la définition du Beau, — de mon Beau') but on the other hand he makes all the Good and the Beautiful his own. The fluctuating dilations of the mind under the influence of hashish probably allow both meanings to co-exist, just as 'des anges de flamme et de glace' survive at the end of the second paragraph and just as 'notre vie tout entière' is spent 'tous les jours'. The pulsation is also expressed in the insistent pattern of recorded beginnings and declared or envisaged endings: 'Cela commença ... cela finira...', 'Cela commença ... cela finit ... cela finit...', 'Cela commençait ... cela finit...'. And this linearity becomes rhythmical circularity just as throbbing in the head provokes giddiness.[11] So 'la fanfare tournant', with the verbal rather than the adjectival form of the present participle stressing the dynamism of the 'fanfare atroce', spins the poet's mind and threatens to leave it, like a burnt-out catherine-wheel, 'rendu à l'ancienne inharmonie'. The energy expended in the process is considerable, and the poison of the drug provides a mask for exhaustion, physical and moral. The latter expresses itself in a parody of Christian prayer, and the possibility of a black mass is not far away:

Nous t'affirmons, méthode! Nous n'oublions pas que tu as glorifié hier chacun de nos âges. Nous avons foi au poison. Nous savons donner notre vie tout entière tous les jours.

It is the poison and the practice of taking it ('méthode') which lead to the claim to know how to die each day, as the bread and wine of the sacraments represent — and for believers are — the body and blood of Christ in daily death. We are prepared for references to religious ritual by mention of 'l'arbre du bien et du mal' as Rimbaud, not alone in this, inaccurately calls it. The epithets 'sacrés' and 'sainte', although charged with ironic overtones at least for the reader, also pave the way. Other terms in the text allow of interpretation in the same direction: 'le corps merveilleux', 'digne de ces tortures', 'cette promesse surhumaine', 'notre très pur amour', 'cette éternité', 'vierges', 'anges'... The assassins at the end, well named, are those who, partaking of the sacraments of this strange religion, kill symbolically in the very process of communicating. There is little need to underline the perversity of this parodic practice or the fact that it is no guarantee of poetry. Yet Rimbaud has made

[11] An interesting comparison may be made with Jules Supervielle's prose poem 'Vertige' in (significantly from this point of view) *Gravitations*. See my study of the poem in *L'Information littéraire*, XXIX, 3 (mai-juin 1977), 146-49.

poetry of it.

If 'Matinée d'ivresse' is set among the fanfares in 'le temps des *Assassins*', 'Barbare' declares itself 'remis des vieilles fanfares d'héroïsme (...) loin des anciens assassins'. These distancing notations may be wishful thinking or reality, but what is certain is the organisation of the cyclical structure, as in 'Matinée d'ivresse', combined with cumulative elements and an open rather than a closed ending. The extraordinary juxtapositions include 'le choc des glaçons aux astres' which seems not dissimilar to the 'anges de flamme et de glace'; and the reek of 'vieilles flammes' is still in the air from the 'débandade de parfums'. Rimbaud still seems to recollect the effects of drugs, 'qui nous attaquent encore le cœur et la tête'. The mingling of ice and fire, though scarcely in a Petrarchan way — 'les brasiers, pleuvant aux rafales de givre', 'les larmes blanches, bouillantes' — prompts an exclamatory 'Douceurs!', 'ô douceurs!', and music of an unspecified kind is heard in this state of euphoric ecstasy. Is it induced, the result of drugs, or is it the benefit of having abandoned them, a symptom of withdrawal? Have we moved here from hallucinogens to 'l'hallucination des mots', or indeed to some quite other kind of stimulus for the vision?

The comparison with 'Matinée d'ivresse' shows that it is impossible to decide. The deliberateness of structure is more apparent in 'Barbare', the title-word itself anticipating in its echoing syllables the swirling repetitions of the text, but the meaning of words and phrases seems even harder to decipher. N critics have worried over 'le pavillon en viande saignante', for example, and come up with n answers. Hackett reviews them (*15*, p.75) and adds a likely candidate of his own, the canopy of the sky. Others have favoured reading 'pavillon' as flag and 'viande saignante' as red — as if that were a remotely satisfactory translation of the violence of the image. So the flags of Denmark, Norway, France and Britain (Union Jack and Red Ensign) have been dutifully waved and further readings — pavilion, sunset, volcano, womb, abattoir — been proposed. Might one not add notions related to the heightened senses of taste and hearing in the roof of the mouth and the pavilion — the flap — of the ear? It would give completeness to the meaning of the otherwise apparently disparate line which implies the other senses: touch for 'la soie', smell for 'fleurs arctiques' (and possibly for the 'viande saignante'!), sight for all of the objects evoked. The line incorporates then the double meaning of 'sens' and enacts a 'raisonné *dérèglement* de *tous les sens*'. For if ever 'l'hallucination des mots' existed, it is embodied in this line, proposed and then withdrawn as it were by the bracketed '(elles n'existent pas)'. Are the 'elles' the 'fleurs arctiques' alone, or those and 'les mers'? Does the pronoun also cover 'la soie' and even 'la viande sanglante'? The vision is snatched from our gaze/smell/touch/taste/earshot. All that is left is the one masculine noun, not covered by 'elles', and so rightly the other words have been written in invisible ink at the end of the poem, reduced to three dots and a trail. Twice said to be deleted, they actually are at the end. But of course syntactically, the further back from 'elles' we go, the more improbable its coverage: it definitely relates to 'fleurs arctiques', may also cover 'mers', could be replaced by 'elle' in the singular to govern the whole phrase from 'la soie' onwards, and is highly unlikely to drive a wedge between 'le pavillon' and 'en viande saignante' which both grammatically and phonetically (villon—viande—ante) are closely bound together. The force of negative entropy (negentropy) in poetry — 'l'ordre improbable' as the poet Lorand Gaspar has called it — should not however be underestimated.[12] At the very least, the 'fleurs arctiques', whether or not they exist in reality (an irrelevant consideration here), are made to exist by being named in all their improbability. That improbablity is then confirmed and compounded by their disappearance in the final declaration of the refrain.

Is this elaborate covering of tracks the sign of an adolescent joke, judicious self-censorship over activities of which he is ashamed, part of his now-you-see-it now-you-don't poetic practice, an anticipation of the surrealistic technique of juxtaposing recognisable realities in unrecognisable combin-

---

[12] *Approche de la parole*, Gallimard, 1978, title of first section. For a brief and clear introduction to the concept, see Rudolf Arnheim, *Entropy and Art: an essay on disorder and order*, Berkeley: University of California Press, 1971.

ations? My answer would be yes to all four, with only the degrees of participation to be debated. The cosmic, totalising vision is derided magnificently, so that one is unsure whether to take the interjections of 'Douceurs', 'O monde', 'ô musique' as Romantic involvement or up-staging sarcasm. Some doubts about the accuracy of the text as copied have been raised and contribute to further doubts: Adam suggests (*2*, p.1005, n.10) that the words 'du vent' should be removed from 'les faux à la pluie du vent de diamants' and inserted in the line above, which would then read: *'pleuvant aux rafales du vent de givre'. Rimbaud would not necessarily reject the awkward 'pleuvant/vent' rhyme, though he might reject the ordinariness of the phrase; and is a 'vent de givre' any more appropriate to the poem than a 'vent de diamants'? The suggestion for the change is not foolish, but there is no way to judge its accuracy, so we must for the time being accept the text as written just as we have to accept our infinite ignorance around the *Illuminations* and get on with analysing the texts. Were meaning determined by the context as it is in ordinary communicative prose, it would be easy to decide that a mistake had been made. It is a measure of the difference between such prose and Rimbaud's prose poems that correction is here impossible. But it is important to remember that what elsewhere is malapropism, illogicality or ineptitude may in the poet's hands become a positive virtue. In so far as Rimbaud is 'l'être sérieux' ('Soir historique') withdrawn from his cosmic visions, he controls his texts and wishes them the way they are. He is reported as saying: 'J'ai voulu dire ce que ça dit, littéralement et dans tous les sens' (*5*, p.80) and wrote on another occasion: 'Ça ne veut pas rien dire' (*2*, p.249).

The likelihood of intentional scrambling of messages and resorting to private coded language grows as the subject becomes more unmentionable in normal society. If Rimbaud's experiences with drugs led him to increased obliqueness and ellipsis, his relationship with Verlaine provoked deviousness and self-censorship of an even greater order. What is done between an adult and a minor in private is subject to legal constraints and so needs a veil of discretion. It will be necessary to draw that veil aside to reveal an important area of Rimbaud's adolescent preoccupations.

A police report of 1 August 1872 prompted by Madame Verlaine's outrage at her husband's suspected activities (quoted *12*, pp.185-86 but wrongly dated 1873 by Petitfils) contains a summary of the situation:

> Comme morale et comme talent, ce Raimbaud [*sic*] âgé de quinze à seize ans, était et est une monstruosité.
>
> Il a la mécanique des vers comme personne, seulement ses œuvres sont absolument inintelligibles et repoussantes.
>
> Verlaine devint amoureux de Raimbaud [*sic*] et ils allèrent goûter en Belgique la paix du cœur et ce qui s'ensuit.

We shall return to the fact that the words 'monstruosités', 'mécanique' and 'amoureuse' appear in that order in the enigmatic poem 'H'. Verlaine's relationship with Rimbaud was considered scandalous, condemned as 'relations infâmes' in the judgement awarding Madame Verlaine a divorce, and gave rise to such jibes as: 'Le poète saturnien Paul Verlaine donnait le bras à une charmante personne, Mlle Rimbaut [*sic*]' or the police reference to Verlaine and 'son *amie* Raimbaud [*sic*]' (quoted *12*, pp.154, 222). Verlaine rejected the accusations vigorously, alleging rather 'les mobiles hautement honorables et sympathiques de ma très réelle, très profonde et *très-persévérante* amitié pour Rimbaud — je n'ajouterai pas *très pure* — fi donc!' (*8*, pp.157-58). One can be homosexual for the highest motives of course, and many societies, including ancient Greece, have considered homosexuality the purest form of love and the naked male the most exquisite beauty. Verlaine and Rimbaud did not live in such a society: the corruption of a minor was, as it still is, a punishable offence, and homosexuality accorded general reprobation.

The nature and extent of their relationship would not interest us were it not for the fact that it was understandably, if often incomprehensibly, reflected in their poetry. We are obliged to be voyeurs to see one aspect, and not the least pervasive, of

Rimbaud the *voyant*. His sense of normal morality, and by all accounts his return to it after his adolescent subjugation to the experiment with Verlaine, leads to a masking of impropriety in writings intended for public consumption. *Une saison en enfer*, the only book Rimbaud actually published, presents the protagonists as 'l'Epoux infernal' and 'la Vierge folle' (*2*, p.102). The former is probably the same as the 'satanique docteur' of 'Vagabonds' in the *Illuminations*. But how many of the female figures in the prose poems may conceal males we cannot tell, yet the possibility cannot be discounted. In private poems, notably when encouraged by the atmosphere of an exclusively male club, Rimbaud indulges in lavatorial fantasies, decorated in the *Album zutique* with graffiti of the most explicit kind. Verlaine, more entrenched in depravity, made less distinction between public and private writings (though he destroyed a collection called *Hommes*, it appears), and his *Œuvres libres* simply move further along the scale which shows clear traces in his *Œuvres poétiques complètes* (from which they are, at least in the Bibliothèque de la Pléiade edition, nonetheless discreetly excluded). To see what Rimbaud was capable of in the genre, one has only to turn to the revealing if unedifying sonnets of *Les Stupra* or the licentious badinages of the *Album zutique* and other titbits (*2*, pp.206-19).

The riddle-poem 'H' has generally been accepted as a prime example of an *Illumination* with sexual innuendoes. If it could be shown that he had somehow managed to read the police report on Verlaine quoted above it would be proved; at least the terms were obviously current. However, one of the most recent interpretations is in a book seeing alchemy as the key to Rimbaud's mysteries, so systematising ideas propounded long ago by Enid Starkie.[13] Equally systematic is the view expressed by Marc Ascione and Jean-Pierre Chambon that Rimbaud's language is coded throughout to hide sexual meanings: 'L'érotisme adolescent n'est pas "une des principales sources" de son inspiration, mais, de loin, la principale' (*27*, p.129).

[13] See David Guerdon, *Rimbaud: la clef alchimique*, Laffont, 1980 (pp.220-24 for 'H') and *17*, pp.104-11. A fuller presentation of my own interpretation is given in *47*, where the sources of the views of other critics are also specified.

Certainly the immediate evidence of 'H' suggests and supports a sexual interpretation, but of what kind? The poet invites us to discover the key to his riddle and decipher 'Hortense'. The first letter of the name provides the unusual title which we cannot help but think stands for something, though we may not guess what. Is is merely for 'Hortense'? The circularity merely compounds the puzzle: how do we break into it? Etiemble and Gauclère, clutching at the second sentence: 'Sa solitude est la mécanique érotique', interpret 'H' as 'l'Habitude', standing for masturbation (cf. *2*, p.218: 'Pauvre jeune homme, il a sans doute l'Habitude!'). Adam stresses sentence three and the word 'enfance' to see 'Hortense' as pederasty. 'Homme' and 'Homosexualité' have also been proposed for their initial letters, but at least one thing seems clear from the text: 'Hortense' must be an object, capable of 'gestes atroces'. That object has to remain under the cover of personification, 'dans sa retraite de coton' (*2*, p.199), for the sake of modesty and decency. Taking 'Hortense' as the penis, as Faurisson first suggested, makes sense of the syntactically straightforward statements of the poem, and is further supported by an expressive piece of army slang, said eyes down in embarrassing circumstances: 'Hortense, couche-toi!', which has been current in this century and may go back to the last. The various concepts described obliquely in the poem then fall into place: masturbation, pederasty, venereal disease, homosexual practices... all carefully dissimulated so as not to shock the reader.

A hidden confessional element stands revealed by a curious feature of the text. The word 'se décorpore' is a neologism and points to its own divided etymology: 'de + corpus'; the unusual word 'clarteux' seems too to split into 'clair' plus a suffix modelled on 'douteux' and/or 'laiteux' (both singularly appropriate in the context), though it has relatively recently been found to have existed independently of Rimbaud. Other words then offer themselves for subdivision: 'novices' into 'nos vices'; 'sanglant' into 'sans gland' (i.e. *glans membri virilis*); last but not least 'Hortense': 'hors tends ce', modelled perhaps on Rabelais's 'c'est beau ce'. Rimbaud was not above such word-play (we have noted the opposite effect of fusion in the 'Sonnet' of 'Jeunesse') nor above such ideas. In 'Les Remembrances du vieillard idiot' (*2*, p.216), the child-narrator recalls his father with touching candour:

> Son genou, câlineur parfois; son pantalon
> Dont mon doigt désirait ouvrir la fente...—oh! non! —
> Pour avoir le bout, gros, noir et dur, de mon père
> Dont la pileuse main me berçait.

He goes on to acknowledge 'le malheur / Du gland tenace et trop souvent consulté' and ends: 'tirons-nous la queue!' In a text intended for publication, however, disguise of such matters was a prerequisite of escape from the attentions of the censor and the law.

There is, however, a higher motive. The riddle is as much a fixed form in prose as the sonnet is in verse: the pattern, if not the arithmetic, must be respected. Yet here we have a poem, not just a riddle, as carefully balanced as the title letter in its syntax, with several binary constructions, and in its subject-matter, with lovers involved in 'passion' (passiveness but also passion) and 'action', matchstick men joining as figured by the capital letter 'H'. In the manuscript (reproduced in *13*, p.149 and *34*, frontispiece and p.167), the title is written as a block capital leaning forward, exactly like the deletion sign used in correcting printers' proofs. 'Hortense', the riddle and perhaps the memory of the experience are to be erased, outdistanced by the poem which stands outside time or, as one might put it in French, 'hors temps, ce'. As Nathaniel Wing rightly concludes: 'The challenge which concludes "H", paradoxically, is a very explicit reminder that meaning in these texts is a function of stylistic structure, and that the "message" is not reducible to the denotative value of words. The system of the text consistently points to its openness' (*35*, p.65).

Other *Illuminations*, notably 'Dévotion', have been interpreted as sublimated homosexuality. It is the sublimation, in so far as it is communicated, that is the consistent striving, whatever the initial experience, that is appreciated by the reader and literary critic. For the experience becomes a metaphor of the striving, and sometimes a metaphor of a metaphor. The freshness and immediacy of the literary effect must not be confused with the experience itself, and that is why we need only a general sense of Rimbaud's various and often extreme experiences in order to situate and relish his organisation of the poems themselves. Even as a child of seven, Rimbaud tells us, he provoked special effects of perception by a willed distortion of his senses: 'Et pour des visions écrasant son œil darne...' (*2*, p.44). He continued to provoke experiences rather than just let them happen to him: 'Je dis qu'il faut être *voyant*, se faire *voyant*', 'je travaille à me rendre *voyant*' (*2*, pp.251, 254). But at the same time his carefully followed apprenticeship in the techniques of versification and his increasing subtlety in awareness of the effects of poetry led him to make of his visions a new and provocative poetics of incongruity.

6. Vision and Blackout

Rimbaud's adolescence was not well prepared for by his mother's domineering authoritarianism. What is for everyone an age of experimentation and discovery became for the precocious poet a time of bewilderment and stress as well. Attracted by the novelties of Verlaine and his circle, Rimbaud lost his moral bearings, the needle veering wildly from the magnetic north of his mother's astringencies. But it is not our purpose to wag a finger at moral aberrations: we need to see how Rimbaud made poetry of his experience.

A time-honoured pedagogical technique known as 'sic et non' (Latin for yes and no) encourages intellectual debate by support-ing an assertion and then, with equal conviction, arguing the opposite. Only at the advanced stage of synthesis and conclusion would any hint of personal feelings enter the discussion, and the perspective of exchanged ideas would reduce their relevance to a minimum. What I have called Rimbaud's 'now-you-see-it now-you-don't technique' is closely akin to this method of exploring ideas and experiences, though because the writing is creative rather than critical, the input of emotion is not reduced but increased by the unresolved tensions of the texts. The dialectic is sequential only because words involve duration: the reader is invited to imagine sequence as simultaneity, discourse as instant, yet sequence and discourse still. The fascination of such complexities survives the passing of youth. Rimbaud is certainly exciting for the young reader, attracted by that rarest of phenomena: brilliant poetry written by someone of his own age, in sympathy with his own crisis. But the adult reader, who may fairly reject as immature the irresponsibility of Rimbaud's late teens, cannot so dismiss the artefacts of exploration, the poems themselves. They are the keen-edged implements used to analyse the world of indissociable dream and reality in which we all live. If gulfs appear between images, leaving us to build bridges of the mind as best we may, they mirror the gulfs in perception and cognition which are our staple. If the texts pattern explorations around the threshold of a here and now, they reflect perhaps instinctively our one access to everything: the present that accompanies us from cradle to grave, instantaneous and multiple in just the same way as Rimbaud's poems are instantaneous and multiple, images of the eternal present.

(Rimbaud's is the kind of poetry in which expression remains exploration, pushing back, through its defiance of the accepted relationship between words and objects, events, actions or concepts, the frontiers of logic and language.) Just as French poetry has become more versatile thanks to his work, to his fulgurations, so our attempts to 'construct a situation' for his truth stretch our imagination and intellectual powers. In the course of his literary production, he pushed perceived reality and heady vision further and further apart, so that in the *Illuminations* the gap is vertiginous.

Some of the metaphors for that abyss, with its perils inevitably accompanied by a sense of tension and exhilaration, have been reviewed in the foregoing chapters, and their intimate links with the form of the poems analysed in striking or representative instances. An important feature of Rimbaud's contribution has emerged: imagery is not used as decoration, mere prettifying of an argument, but is so integrated into the structure of the texts as to make its impact replace argument. We are asked to delight in the very music of scrambled messages. A pattern emerges, both poetic and psychological, but the dangers of over-systematisation are great, and should be resisted with a phenomenon as elusive as Rimbaud.

The radical doubt as to what is vehicle and what tenor in Rimbaud's decontextualised metaphors, noted specifically in connection with 'Marine', is true of all the *Illuminations*. By categorising some metaphorical frameworks as relating to drugs, others to sex, a convenient but falsifying pigeon-holing is practised. Some critics, understandably reacting against the biographical or historical approach, have argued that the texts refer to nothing but themselves, and this methodology has brought enormous gains in awareness of linguistic patterns both phonetic and structural. But words cannot be totally divorced from referentiality, otherwise communication would break down entirely. What seems to defy labelling is therefore the perceiving mind behind the poems, and in Rimbaud's case this shows too many signs of the undifferentiated continuum to allow its products the neat labels which give the reader a satisfying sense of mastery and the consequent tendency towards relegation and dismissal. The turmoil of growing up made the dutiful and successful schoolboy, precocious and pert, reject the adult norms and categories previously imposed upon him. 'Je ne me sentis plus guidé par les haleurs', he writes in 'Le Bateau ivre', and sweeps on, 'taché de lunules électriques' (*2*, pp.66, 68), forerunners of the intermittent flashing light of the *Illuminations*. The oceanic feeling (I borrow Freud's term) is simultaneously a plunge into space and an enveloping security, and the very totality of it leads to an equation with the great religious myths, with a mystical detachment and all-embracing awareness. 'Génie' encapsulates a positively Christ-like projection. If the ecstasies of drugs and sex provoked similar or equivalent states of mind and, more importantly, gave rise to poetry which encompasses disparate realities and a profound sense of vision beyond the material world, the more directly mystical or religious metaphors are close parallels. They do, however, have the advantage of wider acceptability, and so accessibility, and gave rise to Claudel's celebrated formula for Rimbaud: a 'mystique à l'état sauvage'.

There is something disconcertingly spastic, though, about Rimbaud's mysticism: it cannot, it seems, be sustained, nor its moral lessons applied, unless these may be thought to have contributed to his return to the bourgeois life. The breathtaking vertigo of one of the most memorable 'Phrases' leads the mind further and further in space along the tightrope to the vision, the threshold, complete with its festive circus allusion, to a world where the imagination pirouettes in the infinite:

> J'ai tendu des cordes de clocher à clocher; des guirlandes de fenêtre à fenêtre; des chaînes d'or d'étoile à étoile, et je danse.

Yet the very brevity of the poems, and especially of 'Phrases', re-enacts the rapid and often psychologically violent withdrawal from the intense states of heightened awareness. 'Il sonne une cloche de feu rose dans les nuages' ('Phrases' II) is a vivid synaesthetic image and explodes in the mind, leaving indelible traces. The Senegalese poet-president Léopold Sédar Senghor has written: 'Arthur Rimbaud fit exploser la bombe de son délire lucide.'[14] But because such fireworks are essentially unsituated and ephemeral, there is a danger of their being damp squibs, or at least of leaving only the charred debris of the morning after. Perhaps this is inevitable; perhaps indeed it was anticipated by Rimbaud in the 'Lettre du Voyant', in the passage immediately following that quoted in the last chapter where the *voyant* reaches into the unknown:

> Il arrive à l'inconnu, et quand, affolé, il finirait par perdre l'intelligence de ses visions, il les a vues! Qu'il crève dans son bourdissement par les choses inouïes et innommables: viendront d'autres horribles travailleurs; ils commenceront par les horizons où l'autre s'est affaissé! (*2*, p.251)

It is far from certain that one can go further. Cheek by jowl, 'les choses inouïes et innommables' offer the poles of an absolute psychological and poetic rhythm, oscillating between the visions ('il les a vues') and their disappearance. Threshold images hold the balance or reveal that it has been lost. Ellipsis is a formal reflection of a hiatus in the plenitude; the eclipses which occur so often, and notably at the end of poems, are again a structural realisation of that loss. Jacques Rivière, in a book full of sensitive insights, noted 'un motif qu'on pourrait appeler de la lézarde ou de la brèche' (*16*, p.138), and instances dozens of cases where disintegration occurs. It seems a necessary corollary to the existence of the vision, to the existence of the poems, perhaps to existence *tout court*. 'Solde' concentrates its distributing forces on the negative pole of the dialectic, yet just as the 'fleurs arctiques' in 'Barbare' exist before they are annihilated, so all the objects up for sale are lent an existence in

[14] *Elégies majeures*, Seuil, 1979, p.87.

order to be sold off. Loss and withdrawal and departure signify an eclipse of visionary powers, but as with all eclipses, there is always the possibility, the hope, of light returning. As has been said, 'la rupture est le mobile du silence d'où naît notre fascination' (*27*, p.97, n.118). Our imagination penetrates the breaches, sets to work in the margins of the poem.

The dialectic of Rimbaud's prestidigitation shuttles between the poles of verbal creation and destruction. Mallarmé's 'l'absente de tous bouquets' smells different: it is an intellectual essence of flowerness filling the void, a present-absence. No flower is mentioned; it would debase the perfection imagined. Rimbaud has no such cerebral paradigms: his world is messy and in it, as Eliot wrote in the *Four Quartets*, 'every beginning is a different kind of failure'. His are less 'fleurs néantes' as suggested by Paule Lapeyre[15] than 'fleurs anéanties', but the magnetic attraction of the *néant* remains. His poems endure as an absent-presence.

Parenthetically, Verlaine records in his essay on Rimbaud in *The Senate* for October 1895:

> Sur le tard, je veux dire vers dix-sept ans au plus tard, Rimbaud s'avisa d'assonances, de rhythmes qu'il appelait ''néants'' et il avait même l'idée d'un recueil: *Etudes néantes*, qu'il n'écrivit à ma connaissance, pas. (*8*, p.129)

Was the collection perhaps written after all, and given the title *Illuminations* on Verlaine's word? Again we do not know Rimbaud's intentions and probably never shall. The title *Etudes néantes* would nonetheless be singularly appropriate, and more centrally and widely so at least than either of the conjectural sub-titles, 'coloured (or painted) plates'. For the first word, negated by the second, has time to conjure up associations of investigation, work, concentration, music and painting all applicable in different ways to the *Illuminations*. Nor will the age of seventeen mentioned by Verlaine disturb those who are determined to attribute the collection to a later date: at the

---

[15] *Le Vertige de Rimbaud: clé d'une perception poétique*, Neuchâtel: Baconnière, 1981, p.464.

beginning of the same article, he declares of Rimbaud: 'A partir de ce dernier âge [dix-sept ans], il ne toucha plus une plume que pour des lettres privées ou des papiers d'affaires.'[16] Internally, therefore, Verlaine is consistent, and some will argue that he is consistently wrong. His mention of assonance and rhythm in any case leads one to suppose that verse poems of some kind are implied, and since none has survived which post-dates the *Vers nouveaux*, we may assume either that the 'néant' did indeed get the better of the *Etudes néantes* or that something of the idea went into the composition of the *Illuminations*. The result is a bewitching and perilous flirtation with the impossible.

An eminent French critic, Pierre-Georges Castex, has said: 'Je considère que les *Illuminations* demeurent le texte non pas certes le plus obscur, mais le plus difficile à commenter dans toute l'histoire de notre poésie.'[17] In this brief study, I have tried to face those difficulties squarely and suggest approaches to the texts which might bring some illumination in their turn. I am aware how partial my guidance has been, in both senses of the word, with some texts scarcely mentioned. With such a varied and fragmentary collection it could not be otherwise. The abundant commentaries available in good editions and critical studies will make good some of the gaps, and if my signposting proves a stimulus to send readers back to the *Illuminations* themselves in all their tantalising and often truculent fascination, then I too can disappear with this, my own *étude néante*. My equivalent to Chaucer's 'Go, little book' ought really to end with a comma, like Robert Graves' poem 'Leaving the rest unsaid', but I feel that Rimbaud should have the final word, which I also make my own. It is taken from the childish notes first presented by Suzanne Briet as 'Le Cahier des dix ans', the earliest recorded juvenilia of a poet who, as a poet, never reached maturity.[18] It shows an early awareness of what Rimbaud, in a brilliant formulation in the *Illuminations* ('Angoisse'), called 'notre inhabileté fatale':

[16] The first four paragraphs of this article, including this statement, are omitted from all editions of Verlaine's collected writings.

[17] In *Rimbaud vivant* (Charleville), 9 (1976), p.4.

[18] *La Grive* (Charleville), 90 (avril 1956), p.12 of the Cahier.

Il me reste encore des choses à écrire, mais je m'en abstiens sciemment, 1° de peur que je ne te paraisse importun, qui occupe la grande variété de tes affaires, ensuite, si quelqu'un veut essayer par hasard la même chose, il trouve des exemples dans le texte de l'ouvrage, car la matière abonde tellement que c'est plutôt l'artisan qui manque au travail que le travail à l'artisan.

Selective Bibliography

¶ Not a hundred years after his death, writings about Rimbaud exceed Rimbaud's writings by hundreds to one, and the odds are lengthening all the time against seeing them freshly. The following list is selected to try and shorten those odds for the reader, without partisan exclusion, and guide him towards a fuller enjoyment of the poems themselves. Books in French are published in Paris and those in English in London unless otherwise stated.

EDITIONS

(a) of Rimbaud's works:

1. *Œuvres*, ed. Suzanne Bernard & André Guyaux, Garnier, Classiques Garnier, 1981. The most accurate text, with informative and balanced comments. (N.B. The first word of 'Métropolitain' should be 'Du'.)
2. *Œuvres complètes*, ed. Antoine Adam, Gallimard, Bibliothèque de la Pléiade, 1972. The standard edition, to which I have referred for writings by Rimbaud other than the *Illuminations*. Notes tending to be polemically extrinsic.
3. *Poésies, Une saison en enfer, Illuminations*, ed. Louis Forestier, Gallimard, Coll. Poésie, 1973. Exceptional preface by René Char. A good cheap edition.

(b) of the *Illuminations*:

4. *Illuminations: painted plates*, ed. Henri de Bouillane de Lacoste, Mercure de France, 1949. The first scholarly edition, arguing a late dating.
5. *Illuminations*, ed. Albert Py, Geneva: Droz. Full commentaries on each poem. Includes some variants not given in *1*.
6. *Illuminations: coloured plates*, ed. Nick Osmond, Athlone Press of the University of London, Athlone French Poets, 1976. A refreshing (if ultimately unconvincing) reconsideration of the order of the poems, with full commentaries alert to form and possible meanings.

WRITINGS ON RIMBAUD

(a) Bibliography:

7. René Etiemble, *Le Mythe de Rimbaud*, I: *Genèse du mythe*, Gallimard, 1954. Further volumes continue this work of (self-)destruction, the second, *Structure du mythe*, Gallimard, 1952, being a narrative accompanying the bibliography.

(b) Biography:

8. Paul Verlaine, 'Ecrits sur Rimbaud' usefully and cheaply collected in *Fêtes galantes* etc., ed. Jean Gaudon, Garnier-Flammarion, 1976. (Fuller commentary will be found in Henri Peyre, *Rimbaud vu par Verlaine*, Nizet, 1975.)
9. Frédéric Eigeldinger & André Gendre, *Delahaye témoin de Rimbaud*, Neuchâtel: Baconnière, 1974. Rimbaud's schoolfriend's writings on him admirably presented and discussed.
10. Henri Matarasso & Pierre Petitfils, *Album Rimbaud*, Gallimard, Bibliothèque de la Pléiade, 1967. Lavishly illustrated brief biography.
11. V.P. Underwood, *Rimbaud et l'Angleterre*, Nizet, 1976. Detective work about Rimbaud in England. For specialists only.
12. Pierre Petitfils, *Rimbaud*, Julliard, 1982. A full up-to-date life, glossing over some disputed facts (e.g. Rimbaud's participation in the Commune) and not touching usefully on the poetry.

(c) Introductions:

13. Yves Bonnefoy, *Rimbaud par lui-même*, Seuil, 1961. A stimulating view by one (well-informed) poet of another.
14. Marcel Ruff, *Rimbaud*, Hatier, Connaissance des lettres, 1968. A sound, perhaps too uniform, introduction.
15. C.A. Hackett, *Rimbaud: a critical introduction*, Cambridge: University Press, 1980. A most sensitive and balanced book, excellent on the *Illuminations*.

(d) More specialised studies:

16. Jacques Rivière, *Rimbaud: dossier 1905-1925*, ed. Roger Lefèvre, Gallimard, 1977. Collects almost all of Rivière's sensitive writings on Rimbaud. (His *Rimbaud* was first published in 1930.)
17. Enid Starkie, *Arthur Rimbaud*, Faber, latest edition 1973. First published in 1938, revised subsequently, now superseded for much information, but good on obscure sources and alchemical reading.
18. Charles Chadwick, *Etudes sur Rimbaud*, Nizet, 1960. A close critique in particular of *34* below.
19. John Porter Houston, *The Design of Rimbaud's Poetry*, New Haven: Yale U.P., 1963. A readable and rewarding study of the texts.
20. W.M. Frohock, *Rimbaud's Poetic Practice*, Cambridge, Mass.: Harvard U.P., 1963. Emotion recollected in tranquility might summarise the view proposed.
21. C.A. Hackett, *Autour de Rimbaud*, Klincksieck, 1967. The work situated in relation to other major writers.
22. Jacques Plessen, *Promenade et poésie: l'expérience de la marche et du mouvement dans l'œuvre de Rimbaud*, The Hague: Mouton, 1967. Insistence on the theme of movement; an important study.
23. Marie-Joséphine Whitaker, *La Structure du monde imaginaire de*

Rimbaud, Nizet, 1972. Patterns deduced from the themes in the work classified by the elements in the manner of Bachelard; in the line of *30* below.

24. Atle Kittang, *Discours et jeu: essai d'analyse des textes d'Arthur Rimbaud*, Bergen & Grenoble: University Press, 1975. Stress on the ludic elements in the text, with fascinating patterns emerging.
25. Jean-Pierre Giusto, *Rimbaud créateur*, Presses Universitaires de France, 1980. A structuralistic thematic approach, weighty, with insights.

(e) Periodicals:

26. *La Revue des lettres modernes*, série Rimbaud, 4 issues to date (1972-). Consistently serious articles: to be consulted on particular texts or themes and for the bibliography.
27. *Europe*, Nos 529-30 (mai-juin 1973). See especially M. Charolles on 'Mouvement' and the studies by Forestier, Rebourcet/Sancerny and Ascione/Chambon.
28. *Littérature*, No 11 (1973). See especially B. Johnson on 'Conte' and the studies by Felman, Steinmetz and Hartweg.
29. *Revue de l'université de Bruxelles*, Nos 1-2 (1982): *Lectures de Rimbaud*. Includes four studies on the *Illuminations*.

(f) Chapters and articles:

30. Jean-Pierre Richard, 'Rimbaud ou la poésie du devenir', in *Poésie et profondeur*, Seuil, 1955. Sensitive to thematic patterns.
31. Suzanne Bernard, 'Rimbaud et la création d'une nouvelle langue poétique', in *Le Poème en prose de Baudelaire jusqu'à nos jours*, Nizet, 1959. Rimbaud's contribution seen in the context of the development of the prose poem; *the* reference work on the subject.
32. Jean-Louis Baudry, 'Le Texte de Rimbaud', *Tel quel*, 35 (automne 1968), 46-63 and 36 (printemps 1969), 33-53. Linguistic structuralism.
33. James R. Lawler, 'Rimbaud as Rhetorician', in *The Language of French Symbolism*, Princeton: University Press, 1969. The poet as craftsman.

STUDIES OF THE ILLUMINATIONS

(a) The collection:

34. Henri de Bouillane de Lacoste, *Rimbaud et le problème des 'Illuminations'*, Mercure de France, 1949. A milestone in studies on the collection; a late dating argued from graphology.
35. Nathaniel Wing, *Present Appearances: aspects of poetic structure in Rimbaud's 'Illuminations'*, University, Mississippi: Romance Monographs, 1974. A close analysis of about half the poems.
36. K. Alfons Knauth, 'Rimbauds *Illuminations*. *Painted plates* und Philostrats *Images ou Tableaux de platte peinture*', *Poetica: Zeitschrift für Sprach- und Literaturwissenschaft*, IX, 3-4 (1977), 370-97. An intriguing juxtaposition, especially for 'Being beauteous' and 'Fleurs'.

37. Angelika Felsch, *Arthur Rimbaud. Poetische Struktur und Kontext.*
Paradigmatische Analyse und Interpretationen einiger 'Illuminations',
Bonn: Bouvier, 1978. Structuralist approach to selected texts, seeking
Rimbaud's 'logique imprévue', notably in 'Après le déluge' and 'Les
Ponts'.
38. André Guyaux, 'Poétique du fragment: essai sur les *Illuminations* de
Rimbaud', doctoral thesis (5 vols), Université de Paris-Sorbonne, 1981. An
outstanding survey of the state of knowledge of the *Illuminations* with
many valuable contributions. To be published in due course.

(b) Individual poems:

39. Yves Denis, 'Glose d'un texte de Rimbaud: "Après le déluge"', *Les
Temps modernes*, 259 (janvier 1968), 1261-76.
40. Michael Spencer, 'A Fresh Look at Rimbaud's "Métropolitain"', *Modern
Language Review*, LXI (1968), 849-53.
41. Roger Little, 'Rimbaud's "Mystique": some observations', *French
Studies*, XXVI (1972), 285-88.
42. Anne Freadman, 'To read Rimbaud: (b) a reading of "Mystique"',
Australian Journal of French Studies, XI (1974), 65-82.
43. André Guyaux, 'A propos des *Illuminations*' ('Phrases' and 'Villes':
'L'acropole...'), *Revue d'histoire littéraire de la France*, LXXVII (1977),
795-811.
44. Thorsten Greiner, 'Die Verwandlung des Satyrs: zum Verständnis eines
Rimbaud-Textes ("Antique")', *Romanistisches Jahrbuch*, XXX (1979),
100-11.
45. Roger Little, 'Rimbaud's "Sonnet"', *Modern Language Review*, LXXV
(1980), 528-33. On 'Jeunesse' II.
46. André Guyaux, 'Cassure du récit et révélation du sens dans deux poèmes
en prose de Rimbaud: "Conte" et "Royauté"', *Lez Valenciennes*, 6:
'Langages poétiques' (hiver 1981), 81-93.
47. Roger Little, '"H": l'énigme au-delà de l'énigme', *Revue des sciences
humaines*, LVI, 184 (oct. 1981), 129-44.
48. Michael Riffaterre, 'Sur la sémiotique de l'obscurité en poésie:
"Promontoire" de Rimbaud', *The French Review*, LV, 5 (April 1982),
625-32.

CRITICAL GUIDES TO FRENCH TEXTS

edited by

Roger Little, Wolfgang van Emden, David Williams

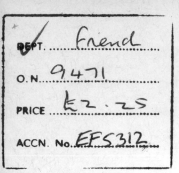